THE
APOCALYPSE
AND
COMING KINGDOM

THE
APOCALYPSE
AND
COMING KINGDOM

KENNETH BEHR

XULON PRESS

Xulon Press
2301 Lucien Way #415
Maitland, FL 32751
407.339.4217
www.xulonpress.com

Paperback ISBN-13: 9781662879357
Ebook ISBN-13: 9781662879364

This book is dedicated to:

My friends, my family, board members, and my church, who have all encouraged me in this effort. In particular, to my wife, who has loved me and shown me how to be a better follower of Jesus Christ, which has made me a better friend, husband, father, and grandfather.

TABLE OF CONTENTS

PREFACE

Are we in the "end of days?" Is this the tribulation, and do we even know what the tribulation is all about? Are the horrible things that the Bible associates with the end of days coming upon us? Is there any hope of escape?

As we get started, I want to commend you for asking this important question and looking for an answer. There have been many books, videos, podcasts, TV programs, radio shows, and church sermons on this subject. Perhaps you are just now trying to get some trustworthy information. Perhaps you have already formed an opinion. Either way, I think you'll find this book interesting.

First, let's start at the beginning: Exactly what are we talking about?

That is a great question! I have intentionally used the word "apocalypse" because it is likely one of the most used and also most misunderstood words in the English language. One of the reasons for the confusion is that the word is not even an English word; it is a transliteration from the Latin word "*apocalypsis*," which actually comes from the Greek. In the Greek as well as the Latin, it is a word that literally means to "uncover" or, better yet, "to reveal."

More appropriate names for the end times than *"The Apocalypse"* would be *"The Day of the Lord"* (referenced 88 times in Sacred Scripture) or *"The Great Tribulation,"* which are the words used by Jesus in Matthew 24.

While there are many opinions on this topic, I do not want to merely give my opinion. The Bible is the greatest source of information on the end times, which many people call *"The Apocalypse."* If you noticed, I added the words *"and Coming Kingdom"* to the title, as what we really need to understand is the coming kingdom of God and how it is different from what we may expect or are currently experiencing.

Whether you are relatively new to "the study of last things" or a seasoned veteran, pastor, or scholar, I promise that you will not be disappointed. We will be using primarily the New King James Version Bible, which was fully released (both the Old and New Testaments) in 1982.

I love teaching from the New King James Version because, while it is a completely new, modern translation of Scripture, it maintains much of the sentence structure and the beautiful poetry of the original Authorized Version, or King James Version. Regarding scholarship, the New King James Version (NKJV) remains faithful to the original Greek, Hebrew, and Aramaic texts, applying the most recent research in archaeology, linguistics, and textual studies, according to Thomas Nelson Publishers, the sponsor and originator of this Bible project.

While you can certainly jump around the chapters of this book, it would be most helpful to begin where all good things begin—at the beginning! I will introduce the topics, characters, and events in a way that should build your understanding of what the Bible actually has to say about the coming Great Tribulation and the coming Kingdom.

INTRO

"THY KINGDOM COME"

For over 30 years, I have been fascinated by and have studied Bible prophecy. One of the best lessons that I was taught years ago is to stick with what the Bible has to say, or at least what people say the Bible has to say. If you follow that advice, like me, you'll stay away from non-Bible sources, including Nostradamus, the ancient Aztecs, Zoroastrian teachings, or even Tarot cards, astrology, and online psychics.

The Bible has a 3,500-year history of faithfully predicting future events. This is called Bible prophecy, and more than 25% of the Bible is actually prophetic.

There are too many churches and pastors who stay away from Bible prophecy. Perhaps they find it too unsettling or too sensational. Many may not have tried to apply what they know about the accepted rules of Bible interpretation. There are actually three principles of Bible prophecy that I follow that align perfectly with the way we interpret the rest of the Scriptures. I may not always mention them, but I will always maintain them.

Three Principles Regarding Bible Prophecy:

1) **Thy Kingdom Come:** These three words are from The Lord's Prayer, and they remind us that the prophecy of the coming kingdom and the second coming of Jesus are integral parts of the prayer that Jesus taught us to pray! Every time we pray this prayer,

also called the "Our Father," these words of Jesus, ***"Thy Kingdom Come, Thy Will Be Done,"*** tell us that there is a kingdom that is coming, and it is something that we should pray for daily.

2) **Prophecy is profitable:** The Bible tells us that ***"all Scripture is inspired by God and is useful for teaching, for refutation, for correction, and for training in righteousness" (2 Timothy 3:16).*** We need to be reading prophecy in order to be complete and to be ready. As prophecy comprises so much of the Bible—nearly one out of every three to four verses—if we ignore prophecy or avoid it, we miss a huge part of the words in the Bible that were given for our benefit.

3) *The Second Coming of Jesus is the "Blessed Hope."* The Apostle Paul spoke often of the second coming of Jesus and called it the "blessed hope." He encouraged the church by saying we should be ***"looking for the blessed hope and glorious appearing of our great God and Savior Jesus Christ" (Titus 2:13).*** We'll talk a little more about this "blessed hope" and His "glorious appearing" a little later in this book, and we'll find that it is something we embrace, not something to be feared.

So, as we study prophecy through the chapters of this book, we'll always remember these three bedrock principles. You will hear me mention them again.

As I mentioned earlier, the title of this book is "The Apocalypse and Coming Kingdom," which intentionally uses a misunderstood word, the word "apocalypse." The Apocalypse is really not an event; it is the ancient title of the last book of the Bible. As you progress through the pages of this book, you'll discover that the terms "last days," "second coming," and "end of days" are terms that are used to refer to events immediately preceding and following what are more appropriately called the tribulation, also known as the seven-year tribulation or sometimes the Great Tribulation.

CHAPTER ONE

COMMON SENSE RATHER THAN NONSENSE

Nearly every day, it is common to see or hear something in the news media or on a social media channel like Facebook or Twitter about the "end of the world," the "Apocalypse," or "Armageddon."

However, when we consider prophecy regarding the Day of the Lord, the end times, or Armageddon, we need to look to the Bible and get our answers from the authoritative source. When we read the book of Revelation, the Book of Daniel (a fascinating Old Testament prophet we'll be looking at from time to time in this book), or any prophetic passage in the Bible, we don't want to interpret the prophetic text based on what may be written in today's newspapers. Current events, the evening news, or political speeches aren't the lenses we use to interpret prophecy.

There has been so much bad information coming from other sources like the newspapers, social media, and even some of the preachers on radio and TV that the mention of prophecy and the second coming of Jesus often creates confusion and ridicule. This was foretold by the Apostle Peter in his second epistle, where he writes,

3 "Knowing this first: that scoffers will come in the last days, walking according to their own lusts, 4 and saying, "Where is the promise of His coming? For since

the fathers fell asleep, all things continue as they were from the beginning of creation." (2 Peter 3:3–4)

Those that are wise (and I hope you are wise) will remember an important saying, "The Bible interprets the Bible." Therefore, when we talk about the prophecies in the New Testament that point to the second coming of Jesus or the establishment of the Millennial Reign (i.e., 1,000 years) of Christ, we will also be looking at the Old Testament to see if there are clues that will help us understand the text more appropriately. Often, we will see that significant end time prophecies are repeated numerous times in both the Old Testament and the New Testament, and by reading and studying all of them, we can uncover important clues regarding their actual meaning.

By the way, this discipline of the systematic study of the second coming of Jesus, the establishment of the millennial reign of Christ, or any last days prophecy is called *eschatology*. The word eschatology is from the Greek ἔσχατος (éschatos), meaning "last," and *logy*, meaning *"the study of the eschaton,"* therefore, *"the study of last things."* This includes unfulfilled Bible prophecy, such as the second advent (second coming of Jesus), the tribulation, the end times, and Armageddon.

To begin, I will provide two keys that I have discovered that are very helpful, if not essential, in understanding Bible prophecy. Let me start this chapter off with a story.

I have had the privilege of serving as a Bible teacher, an author, and in pastoral ministry for over twenty years. This is my second career, so during these twenty years, I went back to school, attended seminary, was ordained, and now I have the opportunity to pastor a church and share the gospel.

As a pastor, one of the questions that comes up from time to time is, "Do you take the Bible literally?"

I don't particularly like the question; however, it deserves a response. The reason I don't like it is that it doesn't have a simple "yes" or "no," and that is true regarding my approach to the Bible in general and prophecy specifically.

Typically, my response is to say that I teach that the Bible is literally the word of God. The Bible tells us that *"all Scripture is given by inspiration of God, and is profitable for doctrine, for reproof, for correction, for instruction in righteousness." (2 Timothy 3:16)*

So, when we read in the book of the prophet Isaiah that a virgin would conceive and give birth to a son whose name would be Immanuel, meaning God with us, we find that fulfilled literally with Jesus being born of a virgin named Mary. We read in the book of Micah that the Messiah would be born in Bethlehem, and when the wise men arrived in Jerusalem and inquired where the King of the Jews would be born, the religious leaders were able to tell them "Bethlehem" because they took the words of the prophecy literally.

However, we also see metaphors and symbolism in the Bible, as Jesus says He is the "good shepherd." That's a metaphor; when Jesus says He is the door, He is using symbolic language.

Often, the mistake of taking things symbolically or metaphorically happens when there is something in the Bible that is particularly spectacular, fantastic, or controversial. These are the very things, being prophetic and spectacular, that people find difficult to believe, or perhaps they just don't want to believe. It is at these precise times that people, including clergy and scholars, assume that these particular Scriptures are not to be taken literally.

We have seen this denial of the literal and obvious even with some of the miracles of Jesus that are documented in all four gospels. For example, when the Bible says that Jesus took a few loaves and fish and fed 4,000 at one time and 5,000 another time, many claim, "This isn't to be taken literally," as if the creator of the universe would find it too difficult to stretch a meal.

Unfortunately, a prophecy (and that is our topic for this book) that is thought controversial or spectacular is often relegated to a "symbolic" or "non-literal" interpretation. This is not an appropriate way to interpret the Scriptures, and more importantly, as a result, many today have not heard even one sermon on the second coming of Jesus or the judgments given in the book of Revelation. These prophetic verses are so spectacular that they are frequently not taken literally. Often, what is not taken literally is not even taught.

However, much of the Bible is prophecy, and to date, all of the prophecies that have been fulfilled have been fulfilled exactly as described. We could say they were fulfilled "literally."

The Bible often gives us clues when a prophecy is to be taken symbolically. Often, these passages include the word "like." For example, in the thirteenth chapter of Revelation, the Apostle John speaks of a beast out of the sea and writes, ***"Now the beast which I saw was like a leopard, his feet were like the feet of a bear, and his mouth like the mouth of a lion. The dragon gave him his power, his throne, and great authority" (Revelation 13:2).*** The word "like" is an indication that the prophecy is using symbolic language. There is a literal fulfillment associated with this beast out of the sea, for sure, but the language that is being used is symbolic.

For centuries, many of the greatest theologians in the church found it almost impossible to believe that in the end times, God would again regather the people of Israel, as was prophesied numerous times in the Bible. The Jews had been scattered to Europe, Asia, and Africa, and later to North and South America; very few remained in the ancient, promised land. Theologians couldn't imagine that God would again turn his attention to the people of Israel and bring them back to the land that he had promised to Abraham and to Jerusalem, the City of David.

But that is exactly what Isaiah had prophesied nearly 2,700 years before it happened. Isaiah says,

> *"Who has heard such a thing?*
> *Who has seen such things?*
> *Shall the earth be made to give birth in one day?*
> *Or shall a nation be born at once?*

> *For as soon as Zion was in labor,*
> *She gave birth to her children." (Isaiah 66:8)*

Israel became a nation on May 14, 1948, nearly 1,900 years after the Roman armies completely destroyed Jerusalem, and the Jewish people that escaped were scattered in what is known as the Great Diaspora.

It was this event that should have convinced many previous skeptics that perhaps all of the prophecies regarding Israel that were yet unfulfilled were all God-breathed and would be fulfilled literally. However, to this day, there are many who continue to not understand end times prophecy because they refuse to take it literally.

Many, if not most, of these end time prophecies deal with the seven years of tribulation, the return of Jesus Christ, and the millennial (1,000-year) reign, and we'll be focusing on these prophecies in detail.

First Key – Take the Literal Meaning When Practical

The first key to understanding Bible prophecy is to take things literally unless it is obvious that they are to be taken otherwise. One of the sayings I like to use is from Dr. David L. Cooper (1886–1965), founder of The Biblical Research Society, who is quoted as saying, **"When the plain sense of Scripture makes common sense, seek no other sense, lest it result in nonsense."**

His actual quote is a bit more scholarly: *"When the plain sense of Scripture makes common sense, seek no other sense; therefore, take every word at its primary, ordinary, usual, literal meaning unless the facts of the immediate context, studied in the light of related passages and axiomatic and fundamental truths, indicate clearly otherwise."*

We begin to discover the literal meaning when we understand that the Bible is a Jewish book, written by Jews for Jews. When the Bible speaks of the Kings of the North (Daniel 11), it means north of Jerusalem. The name "Israel" is mentioned over 2,400 times in the Bible, indicating that Israel is the center of the main story of the Bible.

The word Israel means *"one who struggles with God,"* and God's promises and unconditional covenant with Israel are everlasting. God has certainly provided a pathway for the Gentiles—a pathway to salvation through Jesus Christ—and we can say truthfully that we are living in the Age of Grace or the Age of the Church, but God is not done with Israel.

Second Key – Israel

Israel is the key, and without this key, you will not and cannot understand prophecy. When we read the Scriptures in the book of Revelation, of Daniel, Isaiah, Jeremiah, and Joel, we often see the prophecies speak of *"My people Israel."* Hundreds of references in the Bible to "the law," "Jerusalem," "the temple," "the city," and "the sanctuary" are all direct references to places in Israel. While the judgments of God that are clearly prophesied will impact the entire earth, we should not substitute modern nations or the church when we read of Israel and Jerusalem. This is the key to understanding the true meaning of these prophetic events. The theology that teaches this substitution (i.e., the church for Israel and heaven for Jerusalem) is often called *"Replacement Theology"* and is not helpful in understanding prophecy.

So, remember these two keys! As we begin to look at these Scriptures, we'll recall that the first key to understanding prophecy is to take these prophecies literally. We will take them literally, even when they may be spectacular or include things that may be controversial. And then, we'll recall the second key, which is that Israel means Israel, as God still has a plan for Israel.

CHAPTER TWO
JESUS IN THE CLOUDS

L et's take a look at what most Bible scholars consider to be the *most significant prophetic event* spoken of in the Bible. This event is spoken of in every book of the New Testament, but interestingly, it was a mystery that was not revealed to the Old Testament prophets. In studying the New Testament books of Revelation, 1 and 2 Thessalonians, Peter, and the gospels, combined with the writings of the prophets, including Daniel, Jeremiah, Ezekiel, and Isaiah, we can say that the Scriptures are absolutely crystal clear on not only our future but the future of the human race and planet earth. All of creation is held firmly in the hand of God, and we have no need at all to be fearful of what may be happening to the planet or the nations, neither politically nor economically. The reason we do not worry is because the concluding chapter of human history has already been written in the Bible. We may be worried about what is depicted on the nightly news, but the Lord is not! He isn't worried about elections, COVID-19, or wars because He is still sitting on the throne and there is an ultimate plan. That plan has already been determined, and it is revealed to us in the Bible.

A good place to start is in the epistle of Saint Paul to the Thessalonians. We begin there because most scholars believe that these letters of Paul to the Thessalonians were likely the very first of all of the books of the New Testament.

Thessalonica was a very important Roman colony in what is now present-day Greece. It is a major seaport at the very tip of the Aegean

Sea. In fact, it is this Aegean Sea that separates Europe from Asia, and Paul would often travel between Asia and Europe on his missionary journeys by sailing on the Aegean Sea.

The Apostle Paul's visit to Thessalonica was recorded in the Acts of the Apostles in chapter 17. Acts tells us that Saint Paul was only with the people of Thessalonica for a few weeks, speaking to them in the Jewish temple and having good success among the Greek-speaking Jews and the women but not so much with the Jewish men. Some of these Jewish men were so angry with Paul that they attacked the home of Jason, where Paul had been staying. The Scriptures tell us that some evil and worthless men of the city made up lies about the Apostle Paul and his colleagues.

So, a few months later, when he was in Corinth, the Apostle Paul wrote his first letter to the Thessalonians, after Silas and Timothy caught up with him and told him how well the church he had planted and spent only a few weeks at was flourishing. What I and most scholars find fascinating is that while these new believers in Thessalonica had only spent a few weeks with Paul and were still very new in the faith, Paul spends much of this first epistle talking about the second coming of the Lord and ultimately meeting Jesus in the clouds!

Often the best way to introduce Bible prophecy is just to read it:

> *13 But I do not want you to be ignorant, brethren, con-cerning those who have fallen asleep, lest you sorrow as others who have no hope. 14 For if we believe that Jesus died and rose again, even so God will bring with Him those who sleep in Jesus.*

> *15 For this we say to you by the word of the Lord, that we who are alive and remain until the coming of the Lord will by no means precede those who are asleep. 16 For the Lord Himself will descend from heaven with a shout, with the voice of an archangel, and with the*

trumpet of God. And the dead in Christ will rise first.
17 Then we who are alive and remain shall be caught
up together with them in the clouds to meet the Lord
in the air. And thus we shall always be with the Lord.
18 Therefore comfort one another with these words. (1
Thessalonians 4:13-18)

As I mentioned earlier, we are referring to the most significant pro-phetic event spoken of in the Bible. The return of Jesus Christ is the cardinal truth of Christianity, and it is essentially the ultimate promise made by Jesus.

Unfortunately, many today are like these Thessalonians, unaware, as the Apostle Paul says. They are unaware of this most important of all doctrines. The entirety of the New Testament, beginning with the four gospels and continuing through all the epistles of Paul, Peter, James, and John, ultimately concludes in the book of Revelation with Jesus Christ returning for His people and judging the righteous and unrigh-teous. God's ultimate desire is to be with His people, and that includes a time when He will reward the godly, punish the ungodly, set up His kingdom, and then create the new heaven and the new earth where we will dwell with Him forever.

So, in essence, we are starting our look at Bible prophecy by looking at the "end of the story," and that is a great way to look at what is called the "last days" or the "tribulation." Jesus referred to a specific period during these times as the *"Great Tribulation,"* and we can read what He said in the Gospel of Matthew.

21 For then there will be great tribulation, such as has
not been since the beginning of the world until this time,
no, nor ever shall be. 22 And unless those days were
shortened, no flesh would be saved; but for the elect's
sake those days will be shortened. (Matthew 24:21-22)

As I mentioned before, many want to read these words of Jesus as allegory, believing Jesus to be using symbolic language. But the story that makes the most sense is the actual, literal story of Jesus' return. These are prophetic Scriptures, and all of the prophetic Scriptures referring to the first coming of Jesus were fulfilled literally. As I mentioned, this is the first key to understanding prophecy, and that is to take the literal meaning of Scripture when practical.

Consider, for example, how literally (not symbolically or allegorically) these Old Testament prophecies were fulfilled:

- The Messiah is to be born in Bethlehem.

  But you, Bethlehem Ephrathah, though you are little among the thousands of Judah, yet out of you shall come forth to Me The One to be Ruler in Israel, whose goings forth are from of old, from everlasting. (Micah 5:2)

- The Messiah will be born of a virgin.

  Therefore the Lord Himself will give you a sign: Behold, the virgin shall conceive and bear a Son, and shall call His name Immanuel. (Isaiah 7:14)

- The Messiah is to come from the tribe of Judah.

  The scepter shall not depart from Judah, nor a lawgiver from between his feet, until Shiloh comes; And to Him shall be the obedience of the people. (Genesis 49:10)

- The Messiah would come out of Egypt.

  When Israel was a child, I loved him, and out of Egypt I called My son. (Hosea 11:1)

- The blind will be able to see, the deaf will be able to hear, and the lame will be able to walk.

  5 Then the eyes of the blind shall be opened, And the ears of the deaf shall be unstopped. 6 Then the lame shall leap like a deer, And the tongue of the dumb sing. For waters shall burst forth in the wilderness, And streams in the desert. (Isaiah 35:5-6)

- The Savior would enter Jerusalem on a donkey.

  Rejoice greatly, O daughter of Zion! Shout, O daughter of Jerusalem! Behold, your King is coming to you; He is just and having salvation, Lowly and riding on a donkey, A colt, the foal of a donkey. (Zachariah 9:9)

- The Messiah would be pierced.

  And I will pour on the house of David and on the inhabitants of Jerusalem the Spirit of grace and supplication; then they will look on Me whom they pierced. Yes, they will mourn for Him as one mourns for his only son, and grieve for Him as one grieves for a firstborn. (Zechariah 12:10)

- The Messiah would be valued (betrayed) for 30 pieces of silver.

  And the Lord said to me, "Throw it to the potter"—that princely price they set on me. So I took the thirty pieces of silver and threw them into the house of the Lord for the potter. (Zechariah 11:13)

- The Messiah would be silent before his accusers.

He was oppressed and He was afflicted, Yet He opened not His mouth; He was led as a lamb to the slaughter, And as a sheep before its shearers is silent, So He opened not His mouth. (Isaiah 53:7)

• The Messiah's garments would be divided by lot (dice).

They divide My garments among them, And for My clothing they cast lots. (Psalm 22:18)

These are just ten prophecies in the Old Testament fulfilled by Jesus Christ. Scholars have counted the prophecies fulfilled in the life and ministry of Jesus, and there are at least three hundred more. We believe that these prophecies were literally fulfilled. The prophecies were not to be understood symbolically or allegorically. Bethlehem wasn't just an allegory of a small village; it was and is the City of David. It was Bethlehem where Ruth gleaned in the fields of Boaz, and it was in this exact place, as prophesied by Micah, that Jesus was born of Mary.

Jesus literally rode into Jerusalem on Palm Sunday on a donkey that the Apostles found for Him, and the people welcomed Him as the Messiah, based in part on this literal fulfillment of Zachariah 9:9. This is why we teach that Bible prophecies about the last days, the tribulation, Jesus' return, and other events are to be taken literally, with the understanding that symbols (such as dragons, crowns, horses, and stars) are frequently used to represent reality.

So, getting back to Paul's letter to the Thessalonians and chapter 4 that I quoted above, we should expect and look forward to a time when Jesus will return for His church. At that time, those who have died will be resurrected, and those who are alive will be transformed and given new *"resurrected"* bodies like Jesus. Together, we will all be caught up simultaneously in the clouds to meet the Lord in the air.

If you have never read this before or never truly understood this mystery that the Apostle Paul is telling us, you may need to sit down, take a deep breath, pray a short prayer for illumination, and read it again. It's so amazing that Paul calls it the ***"Blessed Hope."*** In his epistle to Titus, he writes, ***"looking for the blessed hope and glorious appearing of our great God and Savior Jesus Christ" (Titus 2:13).*** The Apostle Paul wrote in this section of his epistle that he didn't want the believers in Thessalonica to be unaware of this truth. It is not unusual for something to be clearly stated by the prophets or by Jesus himself and for His followers to still be unaware. For example, Jesus told the Apostles that He would be betrayed, that He would die, and that He would be lifted up, pointing to the Roman cross and His crucifixion. However, up until the time that Jesus was arrested, the Apostles were often confused and unsure of what Jesus was referring to when He said He was ***"going away"*** and would return for them.

The Apostles were present when Jesus was betrayed by Judas and arrested. Jesus then ***"suffered under Pontius Pilate, was crucified, died and was buried,"*** as the Apostles' Creed summarizes for us. But we also know that our Lord rose from the tomb three days later. He was resurrected with a glorified body that would never be corrupted. Forty days later, Jesus ascended into heaven, and the angels said, ***"Men of Galilee, why do you stand gazing up into heaven? This same Jesus, who was taken up from you into heaven, will so come in like manner as you saw Him go into heaven" (Acts 1:11).*** Since that time, disciples of Jesus have been waiting for His return. I can tell you with certainty that this return of Jesus can happen at any time; it is the very next prophetic event that will happen. Nothing else needs to happen first!

We'll revisit this truth and the timing of Jesus' return in another chapter. But first, we need to take a look at Jesus' response when the Apostles asked Him about His second coming and the end of the age.

CHAPTER THREE

THE DESTRUCTION OF THE TEMPLE

J esus had much to say about the future, the end times, and the signs related to His return. The Olivet Discourse, or Olivet Prophecy, is one of the most quoted Biblical passages and has to do with the future of Israel as well as what we know as the second coming or advent of Jesus Christ and the tribulation. It is found in all three of the synoptic gospels: Matthew 24, Mark 13, and Luke 21. The record in Matthew is the most extensive, so I'll be quoting often, but not exclusively, from the Gospel of Matthew. This entire chapter, Matthew 24, is actually a prophecy by Jesus. He begins by making a comment regarding the destruction of the temple. This happens at the very beginning of Matthew chapter 24.

> *1 Then Jesus went out and departed from the temple, and His disciples came up to show Him the buildings of the temple. 2 And Jesus said to them, "Do you not see all these things? Assuredly, I say to you, not one stone shall be left here upon another, that shall not be thrown down." (Matthew 24:1-2)*

This is just days after Palm Sunday. Jesus had arrived in Jerusalem on Palm Sunday, and the crowds cried out, *"Hosanna to the Son of David! 'Blessed is He who comes in the name of the Lord!' Hosanna in the highest!" (Matthew 21:9)* Then Jesus spent time with His disciples in order to prepare them for what was to come, and ultimately, they came to the magnificent temple that Herod the Great had greatly modified and expanded. It is here that the Apostles casually remark about the grand temple, and as Jesus replies, He prophesies about the soon coming destruction of the temple.

He said to them in reply, ***"Do you not see all these things? Assuredly, I say to you, not one stone shall be left here upon another, that shall not be thrown down." (Matthew 24:2)***

This is why we consider the entire chapter to be prophetic. Verse 2 has already been fulfilled; the rest of the chapter will be fulfilled in what many believe to be the very near future.

In 66 AD, in one of the most stunning fulfillments of prophecy, the Roman general Titus, who would eventually go on to become Titus Caesar Vespasianus, was dispatched to Jerusalem to put down what was known as the First Jewish-Roman War. By 68 AD, the last and most significant fortified city held by the Jewish resistance was Jerusalem. However, in 68 AD, Claudius Caesar Augustus, better known as Nero, committed suicide, plunging the Roman Empire into disarray and civil war, and Titus was recalled to Italy. This put a brief halt to Titus' war against the Jews; however, the Jews, never wanting unity over ideology, became entangled in their own civil war, and fragmented any possible united defense of Jerusalem.

AD 70 and the Destruction of the Temple and Jerusalem

Titus returned to Jerusalem in May 70 AD and began building a siege wall and fortifications to completely surround the city. They soon breached the outer defenses, and the Jewish defenders retreated into the Temple area, which was built similarly, much like a fortress.

Jewish historian Flavius Josephus records in ***"The Wars of the Jews"*** that Titus planned to spare the magnificent and Roman-built temple in Jerusalem. However, one of his soldiers, without orders from Titus and with the help of one of his friends, set fire to the temple through a window. Fire quickly spread through the rooms surrounding the inner temple and the Holy of Holies.

Titus was at the time resting in his tent, and when word got to him that the temple itself was burning, he rushed to the temple in order to put a stop to it. He could not, however, as his soldiers, many of them local mercenaries and Arabs who had a great hatred of the Jews, spread the fire and the slaughter that ensued. Titus thought he could still stop the destruction of the Holy of Holies and gave orders to one of his centurions to restrain the soldiers, but the fire was so great that it ultimately consumed the holy place as well as all of those that were trapped inside.

Historians tell us that this fire and the resulting intense heat melted the gold that lined all of the interior walls of the Holy of Holies. The linings of the walls of Solomon's temple are recorded in 2 Chronicles 3:8 as *"six hundred talents of fine gold."* Six hundred talents of gold at 75 pounds per talent at today's gold exchange rate of $1,700 per ounce would be worth more than $2.4 billion. It's likely that Herod, in restoring, rebuilding, and greatly expanding the temple that Zerubbabel had built after the Temple of Solomon was destroyed in the sixth century BC, may have even added more gold to the finished temple and the Holy of Holies. After the battle, when the fire was out and the melted gold had cooled, the soldiers, many of them mercenaries with a few Roman leaders, began to pry apart the stones of the temple, looking for the gold, prying each stone apart from the foundation, one after another, until the temple was reduced to nothing but a pile of stones. In this way, the words of Jesus—*"Not one stone shall be left here upon another, that shall not be thrown down" (Matthew 24:2)*—were literally fulfilled.

The destruction of the temple and Jerusalem was massive and horrific. Initially, the siege of Jerusalem resulted in Jerusalem being surrounded and cut off from food and water. Thousands died from malnutrition and starvation. The historian Josephus, whom I quoted earlier, records that nearly one million Jews were killed in and around Jerusalem in the battles of AD 70, and over 90,000 were taken captive by invaders. He writes that the Roman legionaries had to climb over the mounds of bodies to get to those still alive in order to slit their throats and run them through with their spears.

Interestingly, and also in fulfillment of prophecy, the early church historians recorded that the majority of the Christians had escaped early as the siege developed, noting Jesus' words recorded by Luke in the nineteenth chapter of his gospel.

> **43 "For days will come upon you when your enemies will build an embankment around you, surround you and close you in on every side, 44 and level you, and your children within you, to the ground; and they will not leave in you one stone upon another, because you did not know the time of your visitation." (Luke 19:43-44)**

This prophecy of Jesus was so well known to the Christians that many, if not all, were able to escape. They saw the prophecy literally being fulfilled when they saw their enemies **"build an embankment around you, surround you and close you in on every side."** So they fled!

The early Christian scholar Eusebius wrote:

> *"The whole body, however, of the church at Jerusalem, having been commanded by a **divine revelation**, given to men of approved piety there before the war, removed from the city and dwelt at a certain town beyond the Jordan, called Pella."*

Bible scholar Adam Clarke also wrote: *"It is very remarkable that **not a single Christian perished** in the destruction of Jerusalem."*

Before we get to the questions the Apostles ask Jesus on the Mount of Olives in Matthew 24, I'd like to draw your attention to Jesus' words in St. Luke's account of what happens after Jerusalem is destroyed in 70 AD.

> **"And they will fall by the edge of the sword, and be led away captive into all nations. And Jerusalem will be trampled by Gentiles until the times of the Gentiles are fulfilled." (Luke 21:24)**

After 70 AD, the Jews were a people without a country. They were literally scattered all over the globe in what is known as the **"Great Diaspora,"** the word *diaspora* coming from the Greek meaning **"to scatter or sow, as in sowing seed."** Until the past century, only a few Jews remained in the area that was known as "Palestine." An interesting historical tidbit: the word *Syria-Palaestina* is the name assigned to this area known previously as Judah and Israel, most likely by Roman Emperor Hadrian in the second century AD after the last Jewish revolt as an insult to the Jewish people. Previously, Palestine, now known as Gaza, was a reference to the Philistines, the ancient enemy of the Jews.

So, we see that this prophecy of Jesus, that Jerusalem will be trampled by Gentiles until the times of the Gentiles are fulfilled, has been partially fulfilled. However, what Jesus meant when He said, **"until the times of the Gentiles are fulfilled,"** will be the topic of the next chapter, "Israel the Fig Tree."

CHAPTER FOUR

ISRAEL THE FIG TREE

S o, let's go on and see exactly what Jesus meant when He prophesied that *"they will fall by the edge of the sword, and be led away captive into all nations. And Jerusalem will be trampled by Gentiles until the times of the Gentiles are fulfilled." (Luke 21:24)*

As I mentioned earlier, the context of these verses recorded by the synoptic gospels (Matthew, Mark, and Luke) is Jesus speaking to the Apostles on the Mount of Olives. He had just remarked that the Temple in Jerusalem would be destroyed and not one stone would be left on another. The Apostles then ask Him a question—actually, three questions:

As He was sitting on the Mount of Olives, the disciples approached Him privately and said, *"Tell us, when will these things be? And what will be the sign of Your coming, and of the end of the age?" (Matthew 24:3)*

The first question was related to the destruction of the temple, and we saw that it was fulfilled literally in 70 AD. As Jesus answers the questions put to Him, we see that the verses that immediately follow are primarily regarding the last two questions. *"And what will be the sign of Your coming, and of the end of the age?" (verse 3)*

We generally understand that the second coming, or second advent, of Jesus is closely related to the end of the age and what Jesus calls the Great Tribulation in verse 21. So, let's jump to verse 29, where many Bibles have a paragraph heading that says *"The Coming of the Son of*

Man" (we'll revisit some of these verses between verse 3 and verse 29 later), and see what Jesus has to say.

> *29 "Immediately after the tribulation of those days the sun will be darkened, and the moon will not give its light; the stars will fall from heaven, and the powers of the heavens will be shaken. 30 Then the sign of the Son of Man will appear in heaven, and then all the tribes of the earth will mourn, and they will see the Son of Man coming on the clouds of heaven with power and great glory. 31 And He will send His angels with a great sound of a trumpet, and they will gather together His elect from the four winds, from one end of heaven to the other.*

> *32 "Now learn this parable from the fig tree: When its branch has already become tender and puts forth leaves, you know that summer is near. 33 So you also, when you see all these things, know that it is near—at the doors! 34 Assuredly, I say to you, this generation will by no means pass away till all these things take place. 35 Heaven and earth will pass away, but My words will by no means pass away." (Matthew 24:29-35)*

While there is still more prophecy by Jesus to learn from the fig tree, this lesson is actually a parable, one of a number of parables in the Olivet Discourse. I enjoy teaching parables because, as Jesus said, they reveal the mysteries of the Kingdom of Heaven. In many ways, these parables bring clarity where otherwise there may be confusion.

So, let's talk about this parable, the lesson of the fig tree. This was Jesus' response to the question, *"And what will be the sign of Your coming, and of the end of the age?" (verse 3)* There are actually two particular instances in the New Testament where Jesus spoke of the fig tree that can provide us with assistance in understanding the parable. The first is the rather interesting and short account where Jesus cursed a fig tree that had leaves but no fruit, and the fig tree completely withered away the next day (i.e., Mark 11:19–20).

The second is a parable that Jesus tells about a man who had a barren fig tree for three years:

> *6 He also spoke this parable: "A certain man had a fig tree planted in his vineyard, and he came seeking fruit on it and found none. 7 Then he said to the keeper of his vineyard, 'Look, for three years I have come seeking fruit on this fig tree and find none. Cut it down; why does it use up the ground?' 8 But he answered and said to him, 'Sir, let it alone this year also, until I dig around it and fertilize it. 9 And if it bears fruit, well. But if not, after that you can cut it down.'" (Luke 13:6-9)*

Both of these accounts speak of the unfruitfulness of the people of Israel, the chosen people. For three years, Jesus ministered to the people, performing miracles, healing the sick, and raising the dead, but the religious leaders rejected Him. They were completely unfruitful. Jesus even used the "three years" as a reference in this parable in the Gospel of Luke.

The parable of the fig tree in Matthew 24 is a direct reference to Israel, both the people and the land of Israel.

Jesus tells this parable between two of the most referenced prophecies in the New Testament. The prophecy of the Son of Man coming on the clouds of heaven with power and great glory is found in Matthew 24. Jesus gives the exact timing of this event as he begins this section, which we just quoted, by saying, ***"Immediately after the tribulation of those days" (verse 29).*** Then, Jesus tells the Parable of the Fig Tree, and it is obvious that Jesus is giving an indication of when these last-day events may happen.

We all understand seasons. We learn that there are four seasons when we are young. The ones we know are fall, winter, spring, and summer. Now that I live in Florida, I have noticed that these seasons tend to run together, but that is not true up north. In Michigan, the state my family calls home, we say we have two seasons: winter and the "4th of July weekend," and while that is a silly joke, we know that there are signs that spring and summer are approaching.

For example, one of the first indications of spring is the appearance of lilies and crocuses. Sometimes they will poke through the snow. Both lilies and crocuses have a very early bloom time, and they are considered the first signs of spring.

In the same way, on the fig tree, when the branch becomes tender and puts forth leaves, you know that summer is near. Jesus is not giving a lesson on horticulture but speaking of the certainty of His coming. Just as the fig tree puts forth leaves, you know that summer is near.

As the fig tree is a symbol of Israel, the fig tree putting forth leaves is a metaphor for the last days. Israel will again be in the land and begin to put forth leaves; its branches will become tender, and we'll see that it is alive, no longer dormant and waiting for its rebirth.

Jesus is not alone in prophesying that Israel will be regathered and that all of the prophecies about the glory of Israel and the righteous reign of the Messiah will be fulfilled literally. For example, from the Prophet Isaiah:

> *He will set up a banner for the nations,*
> *And will assemble the outcasts of Israel,*
> *And gather together the dispersed of Judah*
> *From the four corners of the earth. (Isaiah 11:12)*

And this from the Prophet Ezekiel:

> *Therefore prophesy and say to them, 'Thus says the*
> *Lord God: "Behold, O My people, I will open your*

graves and cause you to come up from your graves, and bring you into the land of Israel." (Ezekiel 37:12)

The most comparable prophecy to the parable of Jesus regarding the fig tree is found in the Book of Jeremiah:

3 Then the Lord said to me, "What do you see, Jeremiah?" And I said, "Figs, the good figs, very good; and the bad, very bad, which cannot be eaten, they are so bad."

4 Again the word of the Lord came to me, saying, 5 "Thus says the Lord, the God of Israel: 'Like these good figs, so will I acknowledge those who are carried away captive from Judah, whom I have sent out of this place for their own good, into the land of the Chaldeans. 6 For I will set My eyes on them for good, and I will bring them back to this land; I will build them and not pull them down, and I will plant them and not pluck them up. 7 Then I will give them a heart to know Me, that I am the Lord; and they shall be My people, and I will be their God, for they shall return to Me with their whole heart." (Jeremiah 24:3-7)

Jesus said very clearly that the regathering of the Jews into Israel would be a sign of His second coming and the end of the age.

What is important to understand is that for hundreds of years, the church, the learned theologians, the scholars, and the priests never truly considered that Israel would ever become a nation again. As a result, even these prophecies of Jesus, Daniel, Isaiah, Ezekiel, and Jeremiah were not taken literally. The Jewish people were thought to have rejected the Messiah, and so the church taught that God had broken His covenant with Israel. But that was not true; God cannot break His promises. In the past few hundred years, many Bible scholars have begun to look again at the Bible and take what it says literally. They were initially a very small minority, but those who believed that the Jews would be gathered back into Jerusalem in the end times, began to be taken seriously.

After World War I, British Foreign Secretary Arthur James Balfour penned a letter to Baron Rothschild, a wealthy and important leader in the British Jewish community, and expressed the British government's support for the establishment of a Jewish home in Palestine. This letter was published in the press and eventually became known as the "Balfour Declaration." This marked the beginning of the modern Zionist movement, which would go from being inconceivable to highly unlikely to actually conceivable after the atrocities of World War II and the extermination of six million Jews in Europe. Then, what was thought to be impossible became possible, and after nearly two millennia, we witnessed the rebirth of a nation.

On May 14, 1948, David Ben-Gurion, the chairman of the Jewish Agency for Palestine, announced the formation of the new state of Israel, and Ben-Gurion became the first Prime Minister of Israel.

Israel was reborn in a day, just as Isaiah had prophesied:

> 8 *"Who has heard such a thing?*
> *Who has seen such things?*
> *Shall the earth be made to give birth in one day?*
> *Or shall a nation be born at once?*
> *For as soon as Zion was in labor,*
> *She gave birth to her children.*
> *9 Shall I bring to the time of birth, and not cause*
> *delivery?" says the Lord.*
> *"Shall I who cause delivery shut up the womb?"*
> *says your God.*
>
> *(Isaiah 66:8-9)*

We all need to pay attention to Jesus' words in another parable about a fig tree. The parable was a response to the questions that the disciples had asked Jesus: *"And what will be the sign of Your coming, and of the end of the age?" (verse 3)*

Let's read Jesus' response again:

> *32 "Now learn this parable from the fig tree: When its branch has already become tender and puts forth leaves, you know that summer is near. 33 So you also, when you see all these things, know that it is near—at the doors! 34 Assuredly, I say to you, this generation will by no means pass away till all these things take place. 35 Heaven and earth will pass away, but My words will by no means pass away." (Matthew 24:32-35)*

Who is the fig tree? Israel! Its branch became tender, and it began to sprout leaves when the Jewish settlers began to resettle in this ancient land of promise. Clearly, the official birth of Israel as a nation on May 14, 1948, is likely a key date. Many people recall the Six-Day War in June 1967, when Israel reclaimed control of Jerusalem, the country's historic capital.

More and more today, scholars, students, and even casual readers of Bible prophecy wonder exactly what Jesus meant when He said, *"This generation will by no means pass away till all these things take place" (verse 34)*.

There are some problems, however, primarily two: First, how long is a generation? And secondly, when does the clock start ticking?

Let's take the second part of the problem first: *"When does the clock start ticking?"* I mentioned the Belford Agreement of 1917 because there were many who said, "This is it; this is the generation!" The reason for saying that is because the United Kingdom was in control of much of the Middle East after the defeat of the Ottoman Empire. There were four waves of immigration of Jews from Europe and Asia between 1881 and 1948, increasing the Jewish population as a percentage from less than 6% to over 30%.

So, it's difficult to fix a starting date. It very well could be 1948, and I like that date myself. Another possible date would be the 1967 date when Israel retook Jerusalem.

The second issue is, *"How long is a generation in the Bible?"* Some suggest 40 years, some 70, and occasionally 100 years. The 100-year time frame is the longest, and it is my favorite because of the context in which it was given. Back in the fifteenth chapter of the Book of Genesis, we read:

> *12 Now when the sun was going down, a deep sleep fell upon Abram; and behold, horror and great darkness fell upon him. 13 Then He said to Abram: "Know certainly that your descendants will be strangers in a land that is not theirs, and will serve them, and they will afflict them four hundred years. 14 And also the nation whom they serve I will judge; afterward they shall come out with great possessions. 15 Now as for you, you shall go to your fathers in peace; you shall be buried at a good old age. 16 But in the fourth generation they shall return here, for the iniquity of the Amorites is not yet complete." (Genesis 15:12-16)*

God said to Abraham that after 400 years He would deliver Israel *"in the fourth generation" (verse 16).* Again, I like this time frame because of the context of Israel coming back into the land, just as God had promised Abraham and was fulfilled as Jacob and his twelve sons traveled to Egypt during the time of the famine and Joseph. At the end of 430 years, in fulfillment of Abraham's prophecy of 400 years, the Israelites (in the fourth generation) left Egypt, as recorded in the Book of Exodus.

Israel is the fig tree; Israel is back in the land! Just prior to telling this parable, Jesus says, "***Now when these things begin to happen, look up and lift up your heads, because your redemption draws near.***" ***(Luke 11:28)***

It is time to raise our heads and look up, because our redemption draws near!

CHAPTER FIVE

THE TROUBLE WITH THE
TRIBULATION

So, let's begin with a quick summary of what we typically understand to be the literal Biblical teaching of the tribulation. We'll get into some of the details in the following chapters. For now, just understand that reading about the tribulation can be troubling because the events are unprecedented. This will be quick, so buckle up!

In Matthew chapters 24 and 25, Jesus is answering the questions put to Him by His disciples about the signs of the time of the end and His second coming. In one passage, Jesus references the tribulation and says,

> *"For then there will be great tribulation, such as has not been since the beginning of the world until this time, no, nor ever shall be." (Matthew 24:21)*

This word "tribulation" is the Greek word *"thlipsis."* It is found 45 times in the New Testament and is typically translated into English as "tribulation." However, it is also translated as affliction, trouble, anguish, and burden. Jesus uses the adjective "great" to distinguish this time of severe affliction, the "Great Tribulation." In fact, in the very next verse, Jesus continues and says,

"And unless those days were shortened, no flesh would be saved; but for the elect's sake those days will be shortened." (Matthew 24:22)

So the word "tribulation" is the more popular term that describes a seven year period that begins when a peace treaty is confirmed among "many" that provides peace and safety to the nation of Israel. The Bible states that this peace treaty will last seven years, but it is terminated halfway through or after three and a half years (Daniel 9:27). So, in this way, often the seven years of the tribulation are broken up into two, three and a half year segments, and the Bible gets very specific by using both days and months even in the same passage. For example, in Revelation, we read,

2 "But leave out the court which is outside the temple, and do not measure it, for it has been given to the Gentiles. And they will tread the holy city underfoot for forty-two months. 3 And I will give power to my two witnesses, and they will prophesy one thousand two hundred and sixty days, clothed in sackcloth." (Revelation 11:2–3)

1260 days divided by 30 days in a month is exactly 42 months, which is three and a half years.

The tribulation begins with the signing of this peace treaty and the revealing of the individual we know as the antichrist. The Apostle John, who is on the island of Patmos, is given this prophecy. The book of Revelation is actually one complete prophecy, from the beginning of the prophecy to the end.

The tribulation marks the final seven years prior to the physical return of Jesus to the earth. His return will be during and at the end of the climactic battle of Armageddon.

The tribulation gets underway in chapter 6 of Revelation with the opening of seven seals. The seven seals are the beginning of a series of sevens: seven seals, seven trumpets, and seven vials.

These initial four seals are known as the "Four Horsemen of the Apocalypse" and feature four horsemen on different colored horses: *white, fiery red, black, and pale,* representing *conquest, war, famine, and death,* respectively. That first horseman, by the way, happens to be the antichrist, who brokered the peace treaty. We'll cover these four horsemen completely in a later chapter of this book.

Throughout these three series of judgments, the Apostle John speaks of many events and individuals under the inspiration of the Holy Spirit and Jesus Himself. For example, 144,000 people from Israel's twelve tribes have been sealed. These 144,000 have an important task. We don't know exactly the details, but they are on a mission from God. Many believe they are preachers or evangelists who are an important part of a huge revival, and many people on earth will come to salvation during the tribulation.

However, the tribulation is a violent and dreadful time, and many of those who come to faith in Jesus Christ will be martyred. They will lose their lives, and John the Apostle writes that he saw in heaven an altar under which were the souls of people who had been slain. They cried out:

> *"How long, O Lord, holy and true, until You judge and avenge our blood on those who dwell on the earth?" (Revelation 6:10)*

Their question and the response that is given are a good summary of the reason for the tribulation. God will sit in judgment over the inhabitants of the earth. God has been patient, and fortunately, many have come to faith. However, evil has often run amok, and God will avenge the righteous.

Revelation chapter 11 introduces two witnesses who appear on the streets of Jerusalem, likely during the first half of the tribulation, who perform miracles, preach the gospel of Jesus Christ, teach prophecy, and condemn the antichrist. These two witnesses are great and faithful prophets. They are two men that some speculate may be Moses and Elijah, representing the law (Moses) and the prophets (Elijah). No one can come against them for 1260 days (exactly three and a half years or 42 months), according to the Bible, before God allows the antichrist to kill them. When this happens, Scripture tells us that the people who dwell on the earth will rejoice, and they actually send presents to each other (Revelation 11:10).

The trials that come upon the earth during the tribulation, represented primarily by the seven seals, seven trumpets, and seven vials, are judgments by God on a world that has embraced evil. The Bible says that those who were not killed by these seven plagues, these judgments by God, would still not repent of *"their murders or their sorceries or their sexual immorality or their thefts" (Revelation 9:21)*. This word that is translated as *"sorceries"* is the Greek word *"pharmakia,"* likely referring to modern-day pharmaceuticals, both prescribed and illicit drugs.

Also, during the tribulation, there are three characters that form an evil trinity: Satan himself, the antichrist, and the false prophet. It will be a time of great deception, and the Scriptures tell us that the antichrist leads a one-world government, and the false prophet leads a one-world religion. During the seven years of the tribulation, Satan gives them both the power to deceive the world through signs and wonders.

During or before the tribulation, the temple will be rebuilt in Jerusalem, and we know this because, half-way through the tribulation, the antichrist defiles the temple, declaring that he is a god and is to be worshiped (2 Thessalonians 2:4).

We are also told that the antichrist requires that everyone take a mark that identifies them as followers of the antichrist, and without the mark, no one could buy or sell (Revelation 13:17).

Occasionally, in the book of Revelation, during the tribulation, we witness events that are going on in heaven. One of the events is what is called the Marriage Feast or Supper of the Lamb, and this is recorded in chapter 19 of the book of Revelation after the church has been taken to heaven and before the return of Christ to earth at His glorious appearing.

One of the final events of the tribulation is what is known as the Battle of Armageddon. This is not actually one battle but a series of battles that involve all of the nations and literally millions of troops that gather to fight against Jerusalem and the returning Christ.

The tribulation ends with this second coming of Jesus Christ, and the description in the book of Revelation is glorious:

> *11 Now I saw heaven opened, and behold, a white horse. And He who sat on him was called Faithful and True, and in righteousness He judges and makes war. 12 His eyes were like a flame of fire, and on His head were many crowns. He had a name written that no one knew except Himself. 13 He was clothed with a robe dipped in blood, and His name is called The Word of God. 14 And the armies in heaven, clothed in fine linen, white and clean, followed Him on white horses. 15 Now out of His mouth goes a sharp sword, that with it He should strike the nations. And He Himself will rule them with a rod of iron. He Himself treads the winepress of the fierceness and wrath of Almighty God. 16 And He has on His robe and on His thigh a name written: "King of kings and Lord of lords." (Revelation 19:11-16)*

These Scriptures tell us that the armies of heaven follow Him, riding on white horses and dressed in clean white linen. Many Bible scholars understand that these individuals riding on white horses and dressed in white linen are the saints of God that return with Jesus to be on the earth for the next 1,000 years, which is the millennial reign of Christ.

In the next chapter, I will introduce you briefly to another great source of many of these prophecies referring to the tribulation, and that is the prophet Daniel.

CHAPTER SIX

DANIEL'S FOUR BEASTS

S o, as we continue through this book on Bible prophecy, we quickly recognize that there is so much unfulfilled prophecy to review that we cannot do justice to it all in just one book. In addition, the signs of the times are growing, and they are growing at an ever-increasing rate. The prophecy about which we wondered how God could bring it about has now become clear. In fact, we are the generation that has seen the greatest sign of the end times: the final seven years called the tribulation and His coming that was prophesied, which was the establishment of the Nation of Israel on May 14, 1948, just as the Prophet Isaiah had prophesied nearly 2700 years before it happened. And it happened just as Isaiah said it would—the nation was born in a day!

In this section of the book, we are going to look at one chapter in the Book of Daniel, Daniel chapter 7, where Daniel has a vision of four beasts. I've selected this passage for a couple of reasons. The primary reason is that we need context. When we look at prophecy generally and prophecy in the New Testament specifically, we need context; we need to compare New Testament prophecy to the prophecies of the Old Testament prophets, like Isaiah, Ezekiel, and Daniel (just to name a few). If we do this, we will be able to better understand the future events, the characters, the nations, and the likely timeline.

There is a saying that the Bible interprets the Bible. The Bible is the story of redemption and restoration, of promises and a people, of trials and tribulations. God is truly the author of the Bible, and He used over 40 human authors, writing in three languages on three continents over 2,000 years, to give us this amazing book. And in the Bible, with a little examination and the help of a concordance, we have all of the references to the symbols, the numbers, and the images that we read in New Testament prophecy.

Let me give you an example of why we use the Bible to interpret the Bible. In the book of Revelation, we read of a beast coming out of the sea that is described in very cryptic and symbolic language:

> *1 Then I stood on the sand of the sea. And I saw a beast rising up out of the sea, having seven heads and ten horns, and on his horns ten crowns, and on his heads a blasphemous name. 2 Now the beast which I saw was like a leopard, his feet were like the feet of a bear, and his mouth like the mouth of a lion. The dragon gave him his power, his throne, and great authority. (Revelation 13:1-2)*

So, if you were just flipping through the Bible and just happened to begin reading in the very first verse of chapter 13, this could be pretty confusing. The language is very mysterious, and how are we to understand this beast with the seven heads and ten horns? Well, while the language may be puzzling, we can use the adage that the Bible interprets the Bible, and we see very similar language in the Book of Daniel.

Let us begin by looking at Daniel chapter 7, and we'll see how it fully explains what we just read in chapter 13 of the book of Revelation. In fact, not only does it explain the symbolism, but it also expands the story and points specifically to the end of days, the coming of the Lord, and the redemption of man.

Daniel's First Vision and Interpretation

So, for a quick background on the Book of Daniel, Nebuchadnezzar, the King of Babylon, the greatest empire of the time, comes to Judah and conquers Jerusalem. He selects some of the royal family, the educated, and the princes of Jerusalem, including Daniel and his friends, Shadrach, Meshach, and Abednego, and takes them as captives back to Babylon. Then, in chapter 2 and in the second year of Nebuchadnezzar's reign, the king had a dream that greatly disturbed him; the Scripture says, *"And his spirit was so troubled that his sleep left him" (Daniel 2:1b)*. And so, the king summoned the magicians, enchanters, sorcerers, and astrologers to not only interpret the dream but also first tell him what he dreamed. These magicians, enchanters, sorcerers, and astrologers could not tell Nebuchadnezzar his dream. Daniel, on the other hand, could tell the king about his dream and its interpretation because he knew the Lord. Daniel then tells him that the dream was about a huge statue, and he describes the statue and the parts of it, starting with the golden head to the feet and toes of baked clay and iron. Daniel then tells Nebuchadnezzar the interpretation of the dream! Daniel tells him the statue represents the four principal kingdoms of the world, beginning with Babylon, followed by Medo-Persia, Greece, and Rome. Of course, Daniel didn't name these kingdoms but described them in a way that provides excellent clues as to their true identities.

Daniel finishes his interpretation with a very important prophecy that is key to understanding the ultimate hope and promise of our God, the Kingdom of God. Let us read those three verses from Daniel chapter 2, verses 44–45.

> *44 "And in the days of these kings the God of heaven will set up a kingdom which shall never be destroyed; and the kingdom shall not be left to other people; it shall break in pieces and consume all these kingdoms, and it shall stand forever. 45 Inasmuch as you saw that*

the stone was cut out of the mountain without hands,
and that it broke in pieces the iron, the bronze, the
clay, the silver, and the gold—the great God has made
known to the king what will come to pass after this.
The dream is certain, and its interpretation is sure."
(Daniel 2:44-45)

This prophecy from Daniel tells us a great deal about the time of the end, the coming of the Lord, and the culmination of this present age.

Daniel says, *"in the days of these kings" (verse 44).* This statement comes just after Daniel's description of the feet and toes being *"partly of iron and partly of clay" (verse 42),* and if they are the same ten kings represented by the ten toes in Daniel chapter 2, then they are likely the same ten kings represented by the ten horns in Daniel chapter 7 as well as the ten horns in Revelation chapter 13 and in Revelation chapter 17.

Most scholars believe this to be the case and understand that these ten kings, or some confederation of ten leaders, kingdoms, or nations, will rise up to dominate in the end days. They don't represent any previous or present confederation of ten kings. The Scriptures tell us clearly that *"in the days of these kings the God of heaven will set up a kingdom which shall never be destroyed; and the kingdom shall not be left to other people; it shall break in pieces and consume all these kingdoms, and it shall stand forever" (Daniel 2:44).*

This kingdom that was to come is not the church, as some have claimed, nor is it any other nation created by man; it is the inner kingdom of heaven, also known as the new Jerusalem, which is described as *"coming down out of heaven from God, prepared as a bride adorned for her husband" (Revelation 21:2).* Scripture tells us that at the end of the seven years of tribulation, the Lord Jesus Christ returns with the armies of heaven, establishes His rule on this present earth, and reigns for 1,000 years (the millennial reign of Christ). After the 1,000 years, the twenty-first chapter of the book of Revelation describes a new heaven and a new earth that will never be destroyed or given up to another people. The Apostle John writes,

> *2 Then I, John, saw the holy city, New Jerusalem, coming down out of heaven from God, prepared as a bride adorned for her husband. 3 And I heard a loud voice from heaven saying, "Behold, the tabernacle of God is with men, and He will dwell with them, and they shall be His people. God Himself will be with them and be their God." (Revelation 21:2-3)*

Now, turning to the seventh chapter of Daniel, we'll see a striking parallel between the vision of Daniel in chapter 7 and the dream of Nebuchadnezzar in chapter 2. It's in these parallels that we have the opportunity to get the interpretation and the prophecy correct.

In this seventh chapter of his book, Daniel wakes and records the vision that he had. This is many years after the interpretation of Nebuchadnezzar's vision; a new king is on the throne: Belshazzar, the last king of Babylon.

Daniel sees four beasts. You could say they are animals, but "beasts" is a better word because they are most unusual: A lion with wings, a bear that looked relatively normal, a leopard with wings that had four heads, and then the most horrible and most terrible of all, a beast with iron teeth and ten horns.

And here we see prophecy being given and then interpreted. Daniel wonders about this strange vision, as you are likely wondering, but the angel comes to him and tells him these beasts also represent the four kingdoms. Daniel previously revealed to Nebuchadnezzar that there would be four kingdoms, so we know the kingdoms: *Babylon, then Medo-Persia, followed by Greece, followed by Rome.*

We also know that the ten horns and toes represent ten end time kingdoms that will be present when the Lord returns. They come out of Rome, the last kingdom represented in the vision and the dream. This is why many look to a revived Roman Empire, which becomes more important just before the Lord returns. Presently, both the European Union and NATO represent significant opportunities to morph into a portion, if not all, of the ten end time kingdoms.

Now, why is this important? Well, the point that is really necessary to make is that when we are looking at prophecy, it is sometimes easy to see these unusual creatures, these beasts, and the symbols and just throw up our hands and say, "I just don't get it," or even worse, begin to assign unusual or more contemporary meanings to the symbols.

For example, there are some who say the bear represents Russia, the lion represents Great Britain, and the leopard represents Germany. However, it is a fool's trap to look at present circumstances and reassign these symbols instead of having the Bible interpret them for us. Assigning these four beasts of this ancient prophecy to four contemporary nations violates well-established rules of Bible interpretation. This is why I called it a "fool's trap," and I'm sorry if I offended anyone.

At the same time, it is equally disappointing and just as foolish when the book of Revelation is dismissed by saying that no one can truly understand these symbols and that they could represent anything—any nation, any person, any system, or any government. That is not how the Bible is to be understood.

In actuality, the prophecy that Daniel recorded in Daniel chapter 2 is so accurate that it boggles the mind. As a result, many skeptics want to reject the historical dating and attribution to the prophet Daniel (i.e., the seventh century BC) and say it must have been penned only after these nations were already known. For these skeptics, it's unimaginable that Daniel would not only get the four empires correctly: Babylon, then Medo-Persia, followed by Greece, and finally Rome. But Daniel could also predict that Medo-Persia would have two aligned kingdoms. In Daniel 8, the Angel Gabriel actually gives Daniel the key to the interpretation. Gabriel says, ***"The ram which you saw, having the two horns— they are the kings of Media and Persia. 21 And the male goat is the*** *kingdom of Greece. The large horn that is between its eyes is the first king (Daniel 8:20-21).* And that first king was Alexander the Great!

Other amazing insights into the prophecy were that the leopard, representing Greece, had four heads.

> *After this I looked, and there was another, like a leopard, which had on its back four wings of a bird. The beast also had four heads, and dominion was given to it. (Daniel 7:6)*

History confirms that after Alexander the Great died at only 32 years of age, his kingdom was carved up by his four generals: Cassander, who ruled Macedon and ancient northern Greece; Lysimachus, who ruled much of Asia Minor; present-day Turkey's Ptolemy, who ruled Egypt and northern Africa; and Seleucus, who ruled much of Alexander's conquest of Asia.

In the eighth chapter of Daniel, there is more detail on the kingdom of Greece and the reign of Alexander the Great. The vision depicts a goat from the west (representing Greece), with a notable horn (representing Alexander the Great), defeating a ram with two horns (representing the twin kingdoms of Medo-Persia).

> *5 And as I was considering, suddenly a male goat came from the west, across the surface of the whole earth, without touching the ground; and the goat had a notable horn between his eyes. 6 Then he came to the ram that had two horns, which I had seen standing beside the river, and ran at him with furious power. 7 And I saw him confronting the ram; he was moved with rage against him, attacked the ram, and broke his two horns. There was no power in the ram to withstand him, but he cast him down to the ground and trampled him;*

and there was no one that could deliver the ram from
his hand. (Daniel 8:5-7)

While the symbols vary from vision to vision, the detail becomes more and more clear. These are different visions that Daniel had, but they point to exactly the same event and the same time period. In this case, the one we know as Alexander the Great is replaced by four!

Now, perhaps some that are reading this do not have an appreciation for all of this history and would really be happy to just find that chapter that talks about the second coming of Christ. Fair enough, I also have a great interest in the second coming of Christ and all of the events that accompany it.

However, these accurate prophecies of Daniel give us both confidence and assurance in the prophecies of the second coming. In addition, the common language, symbols, and nuances of previous fulfilled prophecies speak well to the coming cast of characters in the end of days.

Notice that the worship we see described by Daniel matches very nicely with what we read in the book of Revelation.

9 I watched till thrones were put in place,
And the Ancient of Days was seated;
His garment was white as snow,
And the hair of His head was like pure wool.
His throne was a fiery flame,
Its wheels a burning fire;
10 A fiery stream issued
And came forth from before Him.
A thousand thousands ministered to Him;
Ten thousand times ten thousand stood before Him.
The court was seated,
And the books were opened. (Daniel 7:9-10)

This beautiful picture of heaven is similar to what the Apostle John witnessed as well. Let me quote parts of Revelation chapter 4, and then we will contrast the kingdom of our God with the kingdoms of the earth, with the ruthless and terrible beasts.

> *2 Immediately I was in the Spirit; and behold, a throne set in heaven, and One sat on the throne. 3 And He who sat there was like a jasper and a sardius stone in appearance; and there was a rainbow around the throne, in appearance like an emerald. 4 Around the throne were twenty-four thrones, and on the thrones I saw twenty-four elders sitting, clothed in white robes; and they had crowns of gold on their heads. 5 And from the throne proceeded lightnings, thunderings, and voices. Seven lamps of fire were burning before the throne, which are the seven Spirits of God.*
>
> *6 Before the throne there was a sea of glass, like crystal. And in the midst of the throne, and around the throne, were four living creatures full of eyes in front and in back. (Revelation 4:2-6)*

This is our God; this is His throne room, and we are His people, represented by these elders that worship, honor, and give glory to the Lord. This is a picture of righteousness, of holiness, and of majesty.

But that is not how the Scriptures depict the kingdoms of the earth.

The beasts depicted in Daniel and the book of Revelation are terrifying.

The bear representing the Medes and Persians was to have three ribs in its mouth, likely representing the conquest of Egypt, Babylon, and Lydia, and it was said to it, *"Arise, devour much flesh!" (Daniel 7:5).*

The fourth beast, which we understand to represent Rome as well as the final world kingdom, is described in these words: *"dreadful and terrible, exceedingly strong. It had huge iron teeth; it was devouring, breaking in pieces, and trampling the residue with its feet" (Daniel 7:7).*

While it's one thing to understand who these nations are—Medo-Persia and Greece—we also see that these nations ruled by human rulers are horrible, vicious, ruthless, and terrible.

The Final Beast

Understanding the prophecies of Daniel helps us become familiar with the language that is used to describe these kings and these world leaders. So, when we read John's description of the final world leader, this beast, the antichrist, or in Daniel's terms, the little horn, we can begin to understand his personality, his character, and his rule.

> *1 Then I stood on the sand of the sea. And I saw a beast rising up out of the sea, having seven heads and ten horns, and on his horns ten crowns, and on his heads a blasphemous name. 2 Now the beast which I saw was like a leopard, his feet were like the feet of a bear, and his mouth like the mouth of a lion. The dragon gave him his power, his throne, and great authority. (Revelation 13:1-2)*

It would be confusing, if not terrifying, to read the book of Revelation without first understanding Daniel's prophecies, which describe a beast with seven heads, ten horns, and ten crowns that resembled a leopard, a bear, and a lion. However, we can read this and understand that this final world leader, the one also known as the antichrist, that comes out of the confederation of the ten kings, the ten nations, is just as terrible, just as frightening, and just as horrific as all of these previous world empires combined.

This final world leader is coming! The Bible calls him a beast, and the dragon gives him his power. The dragon, of course, is a common

Bible symbol for Satan. This is why we need our local churches to teach end time prophecy. Knowledge and wisdom are keys, as Jesus warns of deception in the latter days. Providentially, the coming of the Lord is taught in order for us to turn from our wicked ways, to repent, and to come to the Lord. We need to get right with God and fully embrace the One who is soon returning to the earth.

CHAPTER SEVEN
The Two Covenants

This past year, we did a pretty deep dive into Bible prophecy in our midweek Bible studies at the church I have been pastoring for the past five years. Our attendance at Bible study weekly runs between 25 and 40 people, and there were a few that were familiar with some of the prophecies we have discussed so far in this book. Some had studied the book of Revelation and were excited as well that we were dedicating our midweek Bible studies to the study of end time prophecy, called *Eschatology* (a Greek word for *"study of the last things"*).

I've learned that often, especially in teaching Bible prophecy and speaking about the end times and the return of Jesus Christ, it's critically important to make sure we build a good foundation. Good foundations are required if we are to layer truth upon truth.

One of the foundational understandings is that the Bible that we know and study is written in two parts. The first part is the Old Testament. The English word "*testament*" is a translation of the Greek word "*diathéké*," which means "a testament," "a covenant," and "a will." We use the words together often in English when we talk about the "last will and testament" of a person who has died. The word "*covenant*" is typically a Bible word, as it's a sacred trust between two individuals. God made a covenant with Abraham that we read about in the Book of Genesis.

1 Now the Lord had said to Abram:

> *"Get out of your country,*
> *From your family*
> *And from your father's house,*
> *To a land that I will show you.*
> *2 I will make you a great nation;*
> *I will bless you*
> *And make your name great;*
> *And you shall be a blessing.*
> *3 I will bless those who bless you,*
> *And I will curse him who curses you;*
> *And in you all the families of the earth shall be blessed."*

(Genesis 12:1-3)

This covenant that God made with Abram, later to be called "Abraham," meaning "the father of many nations," is the basis of the entire Old Testament. The promise that God would bless "***all the families of the earth***" *(verse 3)* was a prophecy that was ultimately fulfilled in the life, death, resurrection, and ascension of Jesus Christ.

The Old Testament, which we could call the "old covenant," is comprised of 39 books. Together, they form the basis of this original covenant that God made with Abraham, as well as additional promises and covenants that God made with the descendants of Abraham through Jacob (also called Israel), Moses, and David.

The Coming of Elijah

In your Bible, you may have one page separating the Old Testament from the New Testament. Whether it is just one page or a few, most people don't know that there is a 400-year gap between the last book of the Old Testament and the first book of the New Testament. This period is called the *"inter-testamental"* period, also called the ***"400 years of silence."***

As we are studying prophecy in this book, it's important to note that the "400 years of silence" are so called because during those 400 years God was not speaking through His prophets to the Jewish people. The 400 years of silence begin with the final words of the prophecy of Malachi in the very last two verses in the Old Testament, written sometime around 430 BC, where Malachi writes of the Great Day of the Lord.

> *5 Behold, I will send you Elijah the prophet*
> *Before the coming of the great and dreadful day*
> *of the Lord.*
> *6 And he will turn*
> *The hearts of the fathers to the children,*
> *And the hearts of the children to their fathers,*
> *Lest I come and strike the earth with a curse.*
>
> *(Malachi 4:5-6)*

Today, in Judaism, there is a tradition at Passover to have an empty chair and place setting for Elijah. Part of the tradition is for the children to open the front door and see if Elijah will appear for the Passover. In addition, a fifth cup, called the Cup of Elijah, has been added to the order of the Haggadah, a Hebrew word meaning "tale" or "parable." Jewish rabbis are familiar with the prophecy of the coming of Elijah in Malachi, which is the foundation for this tradition. They are, however, wholly unaware that Jesus quoted this prophecy of Malachi and told us that it was fulfilled literally in John the Baptist.

> *7 As they departed, Jesus began to say to the multitudes*
> *concerning John: "What did you go out into the wil-*
> *derness to see? A reed shaken by the wind? 8 But what*
> *did you go out to see? A man clothed in soft garments?*
> *Indeed, those who wear soft clothing are in kings'*
> *houses. 9 But what did you go out to see? A prophet?*

> *Yes, I say to you, and more than a prophet. 10 For this
> is he of whom it is written:*
>
> *'Behold, I send My messenger before Your face,*
>
> *Who will prepare Your way before You.'*
>
> *11 "Assuredly, I say to you, among those born of
> women there has not risen one greater than John the
> Baptist; but he who is least in the kingdom of heaven
> is greater than he. 12 And from the days of John the
> Baptist until now the kingdom of heaven suffers vio-
> lence, and the violent take it by force. 13 For all the
> prophets and the law prophesied until John. 14 And
> if you are willing to receive it, he is Elijah who is
> to come. 15 He who has ears to hear, let him hear!"*
> *(Matthew 11:7-15)*

Between the Testaments

In the four hundred years between the testaments, the Jewish
people saw many conquerors and rulers come and go. In 333 BC,
Alexander the Great conquered the Persians in a decisive battle in
Syria and then brought his troops down to Israel to survey the area.
According to Daniel's prophecy, Alexander the Great was the *"male
goat from the west"* who would decisively conquer the *"ram,"* that is,
the Persian King Darius (Daniel 8:7).

The people of Israel then saw the next part of Daniel's prophecy
literally fulfilled when the four generals, represented by four notable
horns, assumed control of Alexander's far-reaching empire in 323 BC,
when he died at the age of 32 (Daniel 8:8).

At different times, Israel fell under the control of two of Alexander's
generals, known as the *Diadochi* (a Greek word for *"successors"*). The

first was the Ptolemaic Empire, named for Ptolemy I Soter, who set up his headquarters in Egypt. The second was the Seleucid Empire, founded by Seleucus I Nicator, who declared himself to be the Satrap (Governor) of Babylon. Over the next 190 years, Israel would change hands between the Ptolemies and the Seleucids five times, being located on the very important land bridge between north and south, east and west.

Both the Ptolemies and the Seleucids established the Hellenic (Greek) language and culture, as well as Greek cities throughout Syria and Israel. However, the fourth beast prophesied by Daniel was still to come:

> *After this I saw in the night visions, and behold, a fourth beast, dreadful and terrible, exceedingly strong. It had huge iron teeth; it was devouring, breaking in pieces, and trampling the residue with its feet. It was different from all the beasts that were before it, and it had ten horns. (Daniel 7:7)*

The Roman Empire was savage. No empire before them, including the Egyptians, Babylonians, Assyrians, Persians, or Greeks, would be known for their brutality as Rome was. Interestingly, the nephew of Julius Caesar, Octavian, better known as Caesar Augustus, was the one who expanded the former Roman Republic into the vast Roman Empire, establishing what would be known as the Pax Romana, Latin for "Roman Peace." It was named for a 200-year period of significantly less warfare, primarily because the Roman Army was the most powerful in the world. It was peaceful yet savage, as capital punishment was carried out by beheadings (for citizens), and slaves and non-citizens would be crucified, lashed to death, or burned alive.

The Birth of Jesus Christ

The New Testament begins with the genealogy and the birth of Jesus Christ. Most people are familiar with the account of the birth of Jesus Christ, including the journey to Bethlehem and the shepherds and angels. This account is in Luke chapter 2, right after the story of the birth of John the Baptist (who would fulfill the prophecy of the coming of Elijah).

It was Caesar Augustus who ordered that a census be taken of his empire. This is where chapter 2 of Luke's gospel begins, and we read these words in the Gospel of Luke.

> *1 And it came to pass in those days that a decree went out from Caesar Augustus that all the world should be registered. 2 This census first took place while Quirinius was governing Syria. 3 So all went to be registered, everyone to his own city. (Luke 2:1-3)*

The New Testament begins with the historical account of the birth of Jesus. While the Scriptures do not record the exact date of His birth, there are enough clues, including but not limited to the above reference to the decree of Caesar Augustus and when Quirinius was governor of Syria, to ascertain that Jesus Christ was born around 5 BC. The New Testament makes it clear that Jesus is the Christ, which is the Greek word for anointed, just as Messiah is the Hebrew word for the anointed one as well.

In the amazing fulfillment of over 300 Old Testament prophecies, our Lord Jesus Christ was born, lived, died, and rose again. In the same way, this Jesus Christ will return again, just as both the Old Testament and the New Testament prophecies tell us. And here's the thing: there are three times as many prophecies that speak of Jesus Christ's second coming as there are of His first (i.e., 900 vs. 300).

The New Covenant

Earlier, I mentioned the covenants that God had made with the Jewish people in the Old Testament (the Old Covenant). One of the early covenants was with Abraham, which formed the basis for nearly all of the Old Testament, and there were additional covenants that God had made with Abraham's descendants, including Jacob (also called Israel), Moses, and David. The Old Testament prophet Jeremiah prophesied in the sixth century BC of the coming new covenant.

> *31 "Behold, the days are coming, says the Lord, when I will make a new covenant with the house of Israel and with the house of Judah— 32 not according to the covenant that I made with their fathers in the day that I took them by the hand to lead them out of the land of Egypt, My covenant which they broke, though I was a husband to them, says the Lord. 33 But this is the covenant that I will make with the house of Israel after those days, says the Lord: I will put My law in their minds, and write it on their hearts; and I will be their God, and they shall be My people. 34 No more shall every man teach his neighbor, and every man his brother, saying, 'Know the Lord,' for they all shall know Me, from the least of them to the greatest of them, says the Lord. For I will forgive their iniquity, and their sin I will remember no more." (Jeremiah 31:31-34)*

This new covenant is available to all who place their faith in the Lord. It was Jesus who shed His blood to take away the sin of the world, and the Scriptures tell us that anyone who calls upon the name of the Lord shall be saved!

The prophet Ezekiel, who lived basically at the same time as Jeremiah (i.e., the sixth century BC), prophesied as well about the new covenant.

The new covenant is also mentioned in Ezekiel 36:26–27.

> *26 I will give you a new heart and put a new spirit within you; I will take the heart of stone out of your flesh and give you a heart of flesh. 27 I will put My Spirit within you and cause you to walk in My statutes, and you will keep My judgments and do them. (Ezekiel 36:26–27)*

Moving from the Old Testament to the New Testament, readers will notice some significant differences in the landscape. For example, Israel is now occupied by Rome. The Hittites, the Amorites, the Girgashites, the Canaanites, the Perizzites, the Hivites, and the Jebusites are no longer troublesome neighbors of Israel, and the Northern Tribes of Israel are gone and replaced by a mixed-race group (half-Jew, half-Gentile) called the Samaritans.

Just as the Old Testament pointed to the coming of the Messiah, so too, the New Testament points to the second coming, the end of the age, and the return of Jesus Christ. Just as the Old Testament contained the old covenant, the promises of God that were made to Abraham and his descendants, the New Testament contains the new covenant.

There is also a significant difference in the New Testament. It was written after Jesus, the long-awaited Messiah, lived, died, rose again, and ascended into heaven. If there was one word that could typify the old covenant, that word would be "law," as the centerpiece of God's covenant with the people of Israel was centered on the law given to Moses on Mount Sinai. In the same way, if there is one word that typifies the new covenant, that word is "grace."

The Bible tells us that the old covenant contained in the Old Testament has served its purpose and has been replaced by a "better covenant" (Hebrews 7:22). This new covenant was established by Jesus Christ, who is our High Priest, and the Bible tells us it is excellent in many ways.

But now He has obtained a more excellent ministry, inasmuch as He is also Mediator of a better covenant, which was established on better promises. (Hebrews 8:6)

This new covenant and the resulting Age of the Church, also known as the Age of Grace, are keys to understanding Bible prophecy. It is also important to understand that God is not done with Israel, as there are promises to Israel that God has made that will be fulfilled. We will discuss these and more in the remaining chapters.

CHAPTER EIGHT

THE CHURCH AGE

The church age began at Pentecost. In Acts chapter 2, we can read the full account of the birth of the church. The Apostles, along with a larger group of faithful followers of Jesus (known as the 120), were in Jerusalem at the time of the Jewish Feast of the Harvest, also known as the Feast of Shavuot (Leviticus 23:16–22). We know this feast by the name "Pentecost," which is the Greek name for fifty, as it is celebrated on the day following seven weeks from Passover (i.e., 7 days times 7 weeks is 49 days; 49 days plus 1 day is the 50th day).

Jesus had been with His disciples for forty days after His resurrection, and before He ascended into heaven, He told them to wait in Jerusalem for the coming of the Holy Spirit.

> *4 And being assembled together with them, He commanded them not to depart from Jerusalem, but to wait for the Promise of the Father, "which," He said, "you have heard from Me; 5 for John truly baptized with water, but you shall be baptized with the Holy Spirit not many days from now." (Acts 1:4–5)*

That Pentecost Sunday, nearly 2,000 years ago, the Apostles and other disciples were in the upper room when suddenly the Holy Spirit came with a noise like a strong wind. Then tongues of fire rested on each of them, and they began to speak in different tongues as the Spirit enabled them (Acts 2:1-4).

This was the beginning of the church age! The noise and the tongues astounded and amazed the large crowd of people outside because each heard the disciples praising God in their own language. The Apostle Peter preached his first sermon that day to the crowd, and by the end of the day, about three thousand were baptized and added to the church.

When we say the "church age," we refer to this time period we are in presently. Jesus told his disciples that He would build His church (Matthew 16:18), and build it He did! All of us who put our faith in Jesus Christ and believe that Jesus died on the cross for our sins, rose on the third day, and ascended into heaven are part of that church! Whether you are truly a part of the church depends less on where you attend on Sunday and more on who you are, or more definitively, Whose you are!

While the church began on the Day of Pentecost, it overlapped with the previous age, which focused on the Law given to Moses, the sacrificial system, and the temple. There were many Jews who believed in Jesus as the Messiah and continued to worship and fulfill all the obligations of the Law, including the sacrifices at the temple. However, just as Jesus had prophesied, the temple was destroyed in 70 AD by the Romans, and not one stone was left upon another in fulfillment of what Jesus had told His disciples (Matthew 24:2). There has been no temple, and thus no sacrifices, since the previous era ended in 70 AD.

The church that began on Pentecost with the 3,000 that were added and baptized continued to grow. This was a direct result of the power of the Holy Spirit, as Jesus told the disciples,

"But you shall receive power when the Holy Spirit has come upon you; and you shall be witnesses to Me in Jerusalem, and in all Judea and Samaria, and to the end of the earth." (Acts 1:8)

The early church was severely persecuted, first by the Jews and then by the Romans. However, the Apostles, including Paul, who was originally known as Saul and persecuted the church, took the gospel with them as they chose to obey Jesus' words and began making disciples of all nations, baptizing them in the name of the Father, the Son, and the Holy Spirit (Matthew 28:19). While this verse is well known, many do not fully understand the next, as Jesus also mentions the end of the age.

> *"Teaching them to observe all things that I have commanded you; and lo, I am with you always, even to the end of the age." (Matthew 28:20)*

The early Christian church didn't just survive; it thrived! One of the first deacons, Stephen, was martyred around 41 AD, and we can read about that in Acts chapters 7 and 8. A few years later, in Acts 12, King Herod Agrippa kills the Apostle James, the brother of John. Because of the persecution that broke out against the church in Jerusalem, many, if not most, of the early believers were scattered throughout Asia and the Middle East. The Bible tells us that the Apostles stayed in Jerusalem, and Acts chapter 15 tells us that the Apostles met together in what is known as the "Council of Jerusalem" around 50 AD. This first church council was important because the Apostles needed to decide exactly what the Gentile believers needed to do to become faithful followers of Jesus Christ.

Some of the early believers who belonged to what was known as the "party of the Pharisees" declared that the Gentiles must be circumcised just like the Jews and also be required to keep the law. The Apostles Paul and Barnabas argued that God was doing a great work among the Gentiles who had been baptized but had not been circumcised, and the Apostle Peter agreed and said, *"But we believe that through the grace of the Lord Jesus Christ we shall be saved in the same manner as they" (Acts 15:11).*

Then James, the Lord's brother and leader of the church in Jerusalem, spoke up and declared, ***"Therefore I judge that we should not trouble those from among the Gentiles who are turning to God, 20 but that we write to them to abstain from things polluted by idols, from sexual immorality, from things strangled, and from blood." (Acts 15:19-20).***

The amazing spread of the Christian church in the first and second centuries is truly one of the most remarkable events in all of human history. The Jews tried to kill it, the Romans persecuted it, and Nero blamed it for a fire he himself had set in Rome. Nevertheless, the church grew and has continued to grow, to the point that in the past 100 years, it has more than tripled in size. While only Jesus truly knows the condition of our hearts, intentions, and faith, today Christianity remains the largest religious group, with estimates of 2 to 2.5 billion people claiming to be Christians.

According to the Bible, Jesus is and has always been with His church: ***"And He is the head of the body, the church, who is the beginning, the firstborn from the dead, that in all things He may have the preeminence" (Colossians 1:18).***

The End of the Church Age: The Rapture

The church age not only began on a day, the Day of Pentecost, but it will also come to an abrupt end when Jesus returns for the church in the sky. This time, there will be no overlap. There are several names for this event that is described in the Bible, including the resurrection, the rapture, and the catching away. For our purposes, we'll refer to this event as the rapture, which is the transliteration of the word used in the Latin Vulgate Bible, *rapiemur*, found in the fourth chapter of 1 Thessalonians and typically translated in English as *"caught up together."*

> ***16 For the Lord Himself will descend from heaven with a shout, with the voice of an archangel, and with the trumpet of God. And the dead in Christ will rise first.***

> *17 Then we who are alive and remain shall be caught up together with them in the clouds to meet the Lord in the air. And thus we shall always be with the Lord. (1 Thessalonians 4:16-17)*

We will refer again to this most significant event called the rapture, but I first want to spend some time unpacking what the book of Revelation specifically tells us about the church age.

CHAPTER NINE

THE SEVEN CHURCHES OF REVELATION

The book of Revelation (also called the Apocalypse and the Revelation of Jesus Christ) is the last book of the New Testament and the only book of the Bible that has a promise to its readers and those who listen to what it has to say:

> *Blessed is he who reads and those who hear the words of this prophecy, and keep those things which are written in it; for the time is near. (Revelation 1:3)*

While many people justifiably think that the book of Revelation is hard to understand, those who read and study it will not only be blessed, but in time they will also begin to understand it. The main reason for this is that the symbols it contains are frequently explained in detail in a nearby text. For example, in the first chapter, John sees seven golden lampstands in heaven, with Jesus in the middle of them holding seven stars (verse 16). Then, just a few verses later, we read this:

> *The mystery of the seven stars which you saw in My right hand, and the seven golden lampstands: The seven stars are the angels of the seven churches, and*

> *the seven lampstands which you saw are the seven churches. (Revelation 1:20)*

Another reason that the book of Revelation is understandable is because it is logical. The book of Revelation is truly prophecy from beginning to end and primarily sequential from start to finish, with the exception of a few chapters that recap and provide another viewpoint. Finally, and very importantly, it is the only book of the Bible that comes with its own outline.

The outline for the book of Revelation comes early in the book, where John is told by Jesus, *"Write the things which you have seen, and the things which are, and the things which will take place after this"* *(Revelation 1:19).*

Jesus gives John the outline for this book of Revelation. It will contain three major sections:

The first section is "what you have seen," which is the vision he is having of the glorified, risen Jesus in heaven. *"His head and hair were white like wool, as white as snow, and His eyes like a flame of fire"* *(verse 14).* This first section of the outline is just one chapter, chapter 1.

The second section is "the things which are." In the Greek, it says, "the things that exist," the operative Greek word being *"Eimi"* meaning the present state of being. This second chapter of the outline includes chapters 2 and 3, the letters to the seven churches. These churches represent the totality of the church age, from Pentecost to the rapture of the church. We will talk more about these seven churches in just a minute.

The third section is "the things which will take place after this." Another translation says, *"the things which will take place after these things" (NASB).* This third section begins in chapter 4, after the church age, after the church is raptured and removed from the earth. This third section includes chapters 4 through the last chapter of the book of Revelation, chapter 22. These chapters primarily speak of the seven years of tribulation, including the period known as the *"Great Tribulation"* that Jesus speaks of in Matthew 24:21. Chapter 20 introduces the Millennium, a thousand years of peace with Christ as the ruler. We will talk about the Millennium later.

The Seven Churches

The book of Revelation contains a greeting to the intended audience of this amazing prophecy. This intended audience is the *"seven churches which are in Asia" (Revelation 1:4),* and like all the books of the Bible, scholars will tell us that when we try to interpret the writing, we have to view what is being said from the point of view of the intended audience. While this is usually correct, it will limit your understanding of the letters to the seven churches, especially if you only consider the seven churches that existed during John's ministry; and you limit the scope of the entire book of Revelation to these same seven churches.

However, this is not a dilemma if we recognize that these seven churches mentioned by name in the book of Revelation are not only real churches that the Apostle John knew of and was writing to, but they also represent any church that may in fact have very similar characteristics and issues. Most importantly, they are a prophetic look at the entirety of the church age. The prophecy begins with the early church during the days of the Apostles (the church in Ephesus), continues through the Reformation (the church in Sardis), and ends with the modern church (the church of the Laodiceans). This is the church that Jesus rebukes by saying, *"Because you say, 'I am rich, have become wealthy, and have need of nothing'—and do not know that you are wretched, miserable, poor, blind, and naked" (Revelation 3:17).*

This teaching, that these seven churches mentioned in Revelation is a prophecy of the entirety of the "Age of the Church," is best seen in hindsight. We can look back over 2,000 years and see how these churches, their struggles, reputations, and even their names align with the history of the church with uncanny precision. The seven churches taken in order provide an amazing description of seven distinct ages that have specific beginnings and endings. However, if they are not taken in order, the pattern completely falls apart.

Understanding that these churches represent the entirety of the "Age of the Church" provides an extremely helpful tool in understanding the entire book of Revelation and end time prophecy. Scripture makes a distinction between the nation of Israel and the church. The outline we spoke of before, ***"Write the things which you have seen, and the things which are, and the things which will take place after this" (Revelation 1:19),*** will show us clearly that it's after these seven churches (***the things which are***) that the tribulation begins. Revelation chapters 4 through 18 describe events, activities, and judgments happening primarily on earth while the church, the bride of Christ, is in heaven with Jesus at the Marriage Supper of the Lamb (Revelation 19:6-9).

To build on this teaching that the seven churches mentioned in Revelation represent seven distinct ages or developments within the past 2,000 years of church history, we will briefly visit the message to each of these seven churches.

To Ephesus: The Apostolic Church (33 AD to 70 AD)

1 "To the angel of the church of Ephesus write,

'These things says He who holds the seven stars in His right hand, who walks in the midst of the seven golden lampstands: 2 "I know your works, your labor, your patience, and that you cannot bear those who are evil. And you have tested those who say they are apostles and are not, and have found them liars; 3 and you have persevered and have patience, and have labored for My name's sake and have not become weary. 4 Nevertheless I have this against you, that you have left

your first love. 5 Remember therefore from where you have fallen; repent and do the first works, or else I will come to you quickly and remove your lampstand from its place—unless you repent. 6 But this you have, that you hate the deeds of the Nicolaitans, which I also hate.

7 "He who has an ear, let him hear what the Spirit says to the churches. To him who overcomes I will give to eat from the tree of life, which is in the midst of the Paradise of God." (Revelation 2:1-7)

Ephesus was the first church to receive a letter from Jesus dictated to the Apostle John. All of these letters in Revelation were directed to a particular church with a particular application for that church at that time, a teaching for churches throughout the church age, and also provide a glimpse into the 2,000 years (and counting) of the church age!

Ephesus was an important city in the ancient world and a religious, cultural, and economic center. The Apostle Paul, Timothy, his apprentice, Aquilla, and Priscilla all ministered in Ephesus. According to tradition, the Apostle John also served in Ephesus and was therefore very familiar with the church.

First clue: The Apostles

One of the first clues we have regarding the time period that this church at Ephesus represents is the word "apostles." John writes, **"You have tested those who say they are apostles and are not, and have found them liars" (verse 2).** Scholars comment that the word "apostles" is sometimes used in the New Testament as a word for a deceiver seen elsewhere that often speaks well of themselves and even offers impressive credentials (e.g., 2 Corinthians 11:13). However, we note that this word, "apostle," is only used in connection with this first church and gives us the first indication that Ephesus represents the churches present during the Apostolic period.

John writes, *"And you have persevered and have patience, and have labored for My name's sake and have not become weary" (verse 3).* Scholars identify this as indicating that this church at Ephesus was a doctrinally pure church and was even the site of the third ecumenical council in 431 AD. However, often an emphasis on doctrinal purity can make love grow cold, which is exactly what Jesus tells them: *"You have left your first love" (verse 4).*

Jesus mentions the Nicolaitans. This is another clue to the time period this church represents: *"But this you have, that you hate the deeds of the Nicolaitans, which I also hate" (verse 6).* The word "Nicolaitans" is a combination of two Greek words: *nikos,* to conquer, and *laos,* the people, from which we get the word "laity." The early church was very egalitarian in its outlook. While there was structure, it embraced what Peter described as the "priesthood of believers" (1 Peter 2:5-9). The book of Acts in the New Testament tells of the beginnings of the church and tells us that as the Apostles planted churches, they appointed elders (from the Greek word *presbuteros*), also called "presbyters" and "bishops," to be overseers. The Apostle Paul tells Titus, *"For this reason I left you in Crete, that you should set in order the things that are lacking and appoint elders in every city as I commanded you" (Titus 1:5).*

Many scholars understand the works or the doctrine of the Nicolaitans to refer to the time when members of the clergy began to separate themselves from the people (i.e., the laity). Initially, there was no distinction between "the clergy" and "the laity," and Scripture indicates that the preference, at least at the beginning of the Apostolic Age, was for a plurality of elders. The pattern in the New Testament was that every church should have several elders (again, also called presbyters).

So when they had appointed elders in every church, and prayed with fasting, they commended them to the Lord in whom they had believed. (Acts 14:23)

Jesus uses a very strong word when he says He "hates" this doctrine. The doctrine He hates is not whether there is a plurality (a number) of elders, bishops, or presbyters (different words but all referring to the same office) who have been appointed. The doctrine likely being denounced by Jesus is that one group (i.e., the clerics) is becoming dominant and desires to suppress the laity. In contrast, in the New Testament, the most common name for those in leadership positions was "brethren." This word "brethren" refers to all those who are in the faith: women, men, slaves, free, Jews, Greeks, and gentiles.

This first letter to the church of Ephesus represents the "Apostolic Age," which began at Pentecost around 33 AD and continued until about the time of the destruction of the temple in Jerusalem, about 70 AD.

To Smyrna: The Persecuted Church (70 AD to 312 AD)

8 "And to the angel of the church in Smyrna write,

'These things says the First and the Last, who was dead, and came to life: 9 "I know your works, tribulation, and poverty (but you are rich); and I know the blasphemy of those who say they are Jews and are not, but are a synagogue of Satan. 10 Do not fear any of those things which you are about to suffer. Indeed, the devil is about to throw some of you into prison, that you may be tested, and you will have tribulation ten days. Be faithful until death, and I will give you the crown of life.

> *11 "He who has an ear, let him hear what the Spirit says to the churches. He who overcomes shall not be hurt by the second death."*

> *(Revelation 2:8-11)*

Continuing in Revelation chapter 2, the church in Smyrna receives the second letter, which represents the second time period in the Age of the Church. This age would immediately follow the church of Ephesus, representing the Apostolic Age, with little overlap.

The first clue we have regarding the age that this church represents is in the name itself. Smyrna was the name of the church and, additionally, the name of the perfume that is also called myrrh. Myrrh was one of the gifts presented to Joseph, Mary, and Jesus by the wisemen. The song "We Three Kings of Orient Are" tells the story told in Matthew's gospel.

Myrrh had two main uses: perfume and embalming. It was the expensive embalming ointment used by Joseph of Arimathea, who, along with Nicodemus, buried Jesus according to Jewish burial customs.

> *38 After this, Joseph of Arimathea, being a disciple of Jesus, but secretly, for fear of the Jews, asked Pilate that he might take away the body of Jesus; and Pilate gave him permission. So he came and took the body of Jesus. 39 And Nicodemus, who at first came to Jesus by night, also came, bringing a mixture of myrrh and aloes, about a hundred pounds. 40 Then they took the body of Jesus, and bound it in strips of linen with the spices, as the custom of the Jews is to bury. (John 19:38-40)*

The church of Smyrna is closely associated with this sweet-smelling perfume as they represent the "Persecuted Church," and many, while faithful to the end, will in fact be martyred. Some scholars identify this church and time period as the "Church of the Martyrs." One of the other clues as to its identity and time period in the church age is the words that Jesus uses to identify himself. He says in verse 8 of chapter 2, ***"These things says the First and the Last, who was dead, and came to life."*** This is the church during a time marked by suffering, persecution, and martyrdom. Jesus reminds this church that He himself ***"was dead, and came to life" (verse 8).***

The time period of this church age represented by Smyrna is approximately from 70 AD, when the Jewish temple and Jerusalem were destroyed by Titus, until about 312 AD, when Constantine defeated Maxentius and assumed sole control over the Western Roman Empire. Some scholars date the end of this time period as 313 AD, when the Edict of Milan, issued by co-emperors Constantine, Emperor of the West, and Licinius Augustus, Emperor of the East, made Christianity legal throughout the entire Roman Empire.

Persecution against Christians was present certainly before 70 AD, as Stephen, the first martyr, was stoned as early as 34 AD, and persecution surely did not end in 312 or 313 AD, as believers in Jesus continue to be hated and persecuted to this day.

Jesus gives words of encouragement to this persecuted church, knowing full well how many will have to suffer and die.

> ***Do not fear any of those things which you are about to suffer. Indeed, the devil is about to throw some of you into prison, that you may be tested, and you will have tribulation ten days. Be faithful until death, and I will give you the crown of life. (verse 10)***

This church is one of only two out of the seven churches of Revelation to receive a letter from Jesus that contains no condemnation, no correction needed, and no criticism. Jesus tells them, ***""I know your works, tribulation, and poverty (but you are rich)" (verse 9).*** These words should remind the readers of the Parable of the Rich Fool. In this parable, the man thought he was rich and decided to tear down his barns to build larger ones, but Jesus said, *"But God said to him, 'Fool! This night your soul will be required of you; then whose will those things be which you have provided?' 21 "So is he who lays up treasure for himself, and is not rich toward God." (Luke 12:20-21)*

These precious saints who were martyred during this time, and in fact during all time periods, receive the *"crown of life."* This crown of life is referenced here in connection with this church of Smyrna and is also referenced in the Epistle of James.

> *Blessed is the man who endures temptation; for when he has been approved, he will receive the crown of life which the Lord has promised to those who love Him. (James 1:12)*

There are a total of five crowns mentioned in Scripture that appear to be rewards for special acts of Christian service. In this case, the crown of life is for those who persevere, who endure persecution, and who ultimately are martyred for the cause of Christ.

Jesus tells these believers in Smyrna that they are not to be afraid. Jesus had reminded his disciples, *"And do not fear those who kill the body but cannot kill the soul. But rather fear Him who is able to destroy both soul and body in hell" (Matthew 10:28).* The culprit behind their persecution, suffering, and martyrdom was the devil.

Interestingly, Jesus mentions something regarding their persecutions that causes many scholars to opine on its possible meaning. Jesus says, *"Indeed, the devil is about to throw some of you into prison, that you may be tested, and you will have tribulation ten days." (verse 10).* Many scholars teach that the "ten days" may in fact refer to ten intense persecutions that began with emperor Nero and ended with emperor Diocletian at the end of the third century. The time period lines up well with the ten persecutions, even though there is some debate about which ten persecutions should be counted. The more common list of ten includes: *Nero (54–68 AD), Domitian (81–96 AD), Trajan (98–117*

AD), Marcus Aurelius (161–180 AD), Severus, (193-211 AD), Maximus (235-238 AD), Decius (249–251 AD), Valerian (253–260 AD), Aurelian (270–275 AD), and Diocletian (285–305 AD).

Other lists omit some but include *Licinius (308-323 AD) and Julian (361-363 AD)*. These fourth-century Caesars (*i.e., 323 AD and 361 AD*) are after Constantine and the Edit of Milan and therefore past the supposed end of this "age." They could, however, easily be included in the ten, as some propose, as the end date would thus be extended and/or possibly overlap with the beginning of the next church age.

Regardless of whether the Caesars associated with the "ten days" or even the days mentioned in verse 10 do not correspond with ten specific intense persecutions over a period of more than two hundred years, Jesus tells them to **"Be faithful until death, and I will give you the crown of life (verse 10).**

This church in Smyrna serves as a model for all of us throughout the ages. They were ridiculed and persecuted for their faith, and Jesus never promised it would get better. They were told to remain faithful, and God had a reward for them.

To Pergamum: The Church of the Mixed Marriage (313 AD to 589 AD)

12 "And to the angel of the church in Pergamos write,

'These things says He who has the sharp two-edged sword: 13 "I know your works, and where you dwell, where Satan's throne is. And you hold fast to My name, and did not deny My faith even in the days in which Antipas was My faithful martyr, who was killed among you, where Satan dwells. 14 But I have a few things against you, because you have there those who hold the doctrine of Balaam, who taught Balak to put a stumbling block before the children of Israel, to eat things

sacrificed to idols, and to commit sexual immorality.
15 Thus you also have those who hold the doctrine of
the Nicolaitans, which thing I hate. 16 Repent, or else
I will come to you quickly and will fight against them
with the sword of My mouth.

17 "He who has an ear, let him hear what the Spirit
says to the churches. To him who overcomes I will give
some of the hidden manna to eat. And I will give him
a white stone, and on the stone a new name written
which no one knows except him who receives it."
(Revelation 2:12-17)

Continuing in Revelation chapter 2, the church in Pergamum receives the third letter, which represents a turning point in the Age of the Church. This age would immediately follow the church of Smyrna, representing the Persecuted Church, with little overlap.

The reason that there is no overlap is because of one man, Emperor Constantine, also known as Constantine the Great. He is critically important for this time period identified by the church of Pergamum. In 312 AD, when Constantine defeated Maxentius and assumed sole control over the Western Roman Empire, the age of persecution officially ended, and Constantine became the first Roman Emperor to declare that he was a Christian. Many people believe that this time period began in 313 AD, when co-emperors Constantine, Emperor of the West, and Licinius Augustus, Emperor of the East, signed the Edict of Milan, which officially established religious tolerance for all religions. Christianity was the major and sole beneficiary of the Edict of Milan because, within a very short time, Christianity went from being a persecuted religion to the religion of Rome.

We date the end of this time period as 589 AD, as that is the date of the Third Council of Toledo, a Catholic Church council known primarily for the formal adoption of the *Filioque Clause* (i.e., "*and the*

Son") into the Nicene Creed (a point of contention with the Eastern, Greek Orthodox Church).

The name of the church, Pergamum, hints at this time period in the church's history. The Greek word *gamum* is commonly translated as a wedding feast (i.e., ***"The kingdom of heaven is like a certain king who arranged a marriage for his son" (Matthew 22:2)***) and also a wedding (i.e., ***"On the third day there was a wedding in Cana" (John 2:1)***. This Greek meaning of wedding or marriage is used in the English word "polygamy," referring to a marriage with more than one spouse. Many Greek scholars believe that the word Pergamum (per+gamum) refers to a mixed marriage.

Jesus reveals Himself to this church at Pergamum as ***"He who has the sharp two-edged sword" (verse 12)***. A sharp, two-edged sword is referenced in a passage in the book of Hebrews:

> ***12 For the word of God is living and powerful, and sharper than any two-edged sword, piercing even to the division of soul and spirit, and of joints and marrow, and is a discerner of the thoughts and intents of the heart. 13 And there is no creature hidden from His sight, but all things are naked and open to the eyes of Him to whom we must give account.***
>
> ***(Hebrews 4:12-13)***

Over time, cultures, customs, belief systems, doctrines, and practices can mix and blend together, but the word of God is able to discern the difference. This title that Jesus uses for Himself is a reminder that the word of God is the final authority in all matters of faith. There is little doubt that pagan practices and culture mixed with the Christian faith during this time period. The term that is often used regarding this phenomenon is syncretism. It can be defined as the amalgamation of different religions, beliefs, and cultures.

Jesus commends this church: ***"I know your works, and where you dwell, where Satan's throne is. And you hold fast to My name,"* (verse 13).** Pergamum was an extremely religious city and a stronghold of satanic power. Pergamum had temples to four of the twelve major Greek deities (said to reside on Mount Olympus): Dionysus, Athena, Demeter, and Zeus. The Christians living in Pergamum were a small and often persecuted minority among a very religious and very pagan people.

This throne of Satan mentioned in the Scripture is thought to be the altar of Zeus. This altar was forgotten among the ruins of this ancient city of Pergamum until 1864, when a German engineer named Carl Humann found it while excavating the ruins of the city.

Later, Adolf Hitler, Germany's new chancellor, used this altar, this satanic throne, as inspiration for the design of his colossal, 400,000-seat stadium in Nuremberg, built for the 1936 Olympics. It's interesting how what may have seemed like a minor historical artifact would have such a prominent role in the 20th century.

The church of Pergamum receives the brief commendation referenced above and mentions an otherwise unknown martyr, Antipas. Jesus then addresses some things that He has against them.

Two specific teachings are mentioned by Jesus that also provide insight into the age that Pergamum represents. The first is the teaching of Balaam, and the second is the teaching of the Nicolaitans.

The Teaching of Balaam

This teaching of Balaam, referenced in connection with the church of Pergamum in Revelation 2:14, is a warning about false teachers and about compromise. Balaam was a pagan prophet who gave advice to Moab King Balak on the best way to weaken the people of Israel. Balaam encouraged marriage between the Israelite men and Moabite and Midianite women that ultimately brought Israel into idolatry and judgment upon themselves (Numbers 25:1–9). This is what Jesus refers to as putting *"a stumbling block before the children of Israel, to eat things sacrificed to idols, and to commit sexual immorality" (verse 14).*

The Doctrine of the Nicolaitans

It was mentioned earlier in the letter to the Ephesians that Jesus hates the works of the Nicolaitans and that the word Nicolaitans is a combination of two Greek words: *nikos*, to conquer, and *laos*, the people, from which we get the word "laity." While the early church was very egalitarian and classless, by the fourth century, the laity had no voice in church matters. A hierarchy had developed that placed all of the power with the bishops and the senior bishops, called patriarchs. An official organizational structure called **Pentarchy** (from the Greek words for "five" and "to rule") was formulated by Emperor Justinian I (527–565) and decreed that five major centers: Jerusalem, Alexandria, Constantinople, Antioch, and Rome would rule and have jurisdiction.

Not only did the clergy and these bishops *"lord it over" (Matthew 20:25)* the rest of the people, but over time, the laity began to think of themselves and be treated as unworthy. Ultimately, the western church, with their bishop in Rome, who would become known as the pope, would separate from the other four patriarchs in what is still known to this day as the Eastern Orthodox Church.

To Thyatira: The Church of Rome (589 AD to the Rapture)

18 "And to the angel of the church in Thyatira write,

'These things says the Son of God, who has eyes like a flame of fire, and His feet like fine brass: 19 "I know your works, love, service, faith, and your patience; and as for your works, the last are more than the first. 20 Nevertheless I have a few things against you, because you allow that woman Jezebel, who calls herself a

prophetess, to teach and seduce My servants to commit sexual immorality and eat things sacrificed to idols. 21 And I gave her time to repent of her sexual immorality, and she did not repent. 22 Indeed I will cast her into a sickbed, and those who commit adultery with her into great tribulation, unless they repent of their deeds. 23 I will kill her children with death, and all the churches shall know that I am He who searches the minds and hearts. And I will give to each one of you according to your works. 24 "Now to you I say, and to the rest in Thyatira, as many as do not have this doctrine, who have not known the depths of Satan, as they say, I will put on you no other burden. 25 But hold fast what you have till I come. 26 And he who overcomes, and keeps My works until the end, to him I will give power over the nations— 27 'He shall rule them with a rod of iron; They shall be dashed to pieces like the potter's vessels'—as I also have received from My Father; 28 and I will give him the morning star. 29 "He who has an ear, let him hear what the Spirit says to the churches." '
(Revelation 2:18-29)

Continuing now to the end of chapter 2 in Revelation, the church in Thyatira is the fourth of the seven churches and now represents the timeline of a church that will be present when Jesus returns for the church at the time of the rapture. We date this church from the end of the previous church period, around 589 AD, at the end of the sixth century. By this time, the Church of Rome represented, for all practical purposes, both a civil as well as a religious authority throughout nearly all of Europe.

For those with a Roman Catholic background, this teaching on this church and time period may appear offensive. However, we need to embrace both the good and the bad, as Jesus has some very good things to say about the church of Thyatira. This church most likely represents the Church of Rome, as did the church of Pergamos, which preceded it. However, the next church letter is to the church of Sardis, and (spoiler alert!) we will see that this represents the church of the Reformation, and Jesus has nothing good to say about Sardis.

Like the preceding churches, the first clue we have regarding the age that this church represents is in the name itself: "Thyatira," a name that means *"odor of affliction."* Some readers may have heard that many Bible scholars have said that this word, Thyatira, means "continued sacrifice," possibly because it fits well with the Roman Catholic concept of the sacrifice of the mass. However, I'll stick with my trusted Strong's concordance of the Greek, Strong's G2363, which says that the appropriate Greek translation is "odor of affliction."

It could be that the "odor of affliction" well describes the state of the church of Rome, particularly during the Middle Ages from the 5th to the 15th centuries. The church of Thyatira received the longest of the letters from Jesus, containing both strong commendations regarding their love, service, faith, and patience, as well as somber condemnations for the conditions that would prevail, resulting symbolically from this woman named Jezebel, *"who calls herself a prophetess, to teach and seduce My servants to commit sexual immorality and eat things sacrificed to idols" (verse 20).*

First, regarding the commendations, few would argue against the many great and good works of the Church of Rome. For centuries, the Church of Rome has provided for the needs of others. We owe our hospitals, educational facilities, hospice centers, rescue missions, orphanages, and schools, at least in the west, to the Church of Rome's calling and charity. Notice what the prophecy here in verse 19 says regarding her works: *"The last are more than the first."*

And while many give the Church of Rome their due credit for these many good works, many must also admit to much of the abuse, the "odor of affliction," caused by this same church. Affliction can also mean illness, which is what Jesus mentions as the result of their infidelity.

22 Indeed I will cast her into a sickbed, and those who commit adultery with her into great tribulation, unless they repent of their deeds. 23 I will kill her children with death (verses 22–23).

This brings us to this woman, Jezebel, whom Jesus said was being tolerated by the church.

The evil queen Jezebel is referenced in both 1 and 2 Kings. She was the pagan wife of King Ahab of Israel, who not only seduced the people of God into worshipping idols but was also culpable for manipulating weak King Ahab into abusing his power as king and protector of his people. Jezebel was notoriously wicked and so infamous that I remind those in my Bible studies that no one names their daughter "Jezebel." Reading the stories of Jezebel in the Bible portrays an evil queen who was power-hungry, wicked, and contemptuous. She knew no limits when it came to ruling with a heavy hand and with violence and intimidation.

There is a well-known saying that *"power corrupts, and absolute power corrupts absolutely."* History tells a story of abuse by the hierarchy of the Church of Rome that was little different from that of previous Roman emperors, despot kings, and tyrannical monarchs.

The one thing that the Church of Rome had above all else was power. The Church of Rome was not only the only approved religious system in Rome; it was also the Catholic Church, the word catholic meaning universal. Anyone who opposed the teachings of the church, including the primacy of the pope, became an enemy of the church, and their teachings were declared anathema, meaning cursed or damned.

All who stood up to the abuses of the church or refused to acknowledge the hierarchy of the church were persecuted. By the Middle Ages, nearly all of the higher offices of the church (e.g., Pope, Cardinal, Bishop, and Abbot) were bought and paid for by families eager to have their family members installed in these honored and powerful ecclesiastical positions. The Bible calls this the sin of Simony, named for Simon in the Bible, who wanted to pay money to the Apostles to receive the gift and power of the Holy Spirit (Acts 8:18). Many faithful Christians were executed as "heretics," reminiscent of the ways of the evil rulers of Israel, King Ahab and the wicked queen Jezebel.

Long before the Protestant Reformation and the publication of Martin Luther's Ninety-five Theses in 1517, men like John Wycliff of England (1320–1384) and Jan Hus (1369–1415) were persecuted by the Church of Rome. John Wycliff, who translated the Bible into English, was never officially excommunicated by Rome; however, long after his death, the Council of Constance ruled that his body should be exhumed and his bones burned, identifying Wycliff as a common heretic. This same council invited Jan Hus and Jerome of Prague (1379–1416), a Czech reformer, to the city of Constance in present day Germany, to explain their views that were similar to Wycliff's, including the authority of the Bible over the traditions of the church, the abuse arising from the office of the pope and other church offices, and the sale of indulgences. The Council tried Hus and Jerome for heresy, urging them both to recant these teachings of Wycliff as well as their own, but both men refused, were condemned by the Council, and were burned at the stake on July 6, 1415.

Note that in this letter to Thyatira, Jesus delivers some good news after a very somber condemnation. Jesus says, "**Now to you I say, and to the rest in Thyatira, as many as do not have this doctrine, who have not known the depths of Satan, as they say, I will put on you no other burden. 25 But hold fast what you have till I come**" (Revelation 2:24-25).

This is the first of the seven churches of Revelation in which Jesus includes the words *"till I come" (verse 25)*, indicating the time period for this church continues until Jesus returns in the rapture of the church. Many modern-day Catholics never held some of these teachings that Jesus was against, from which He called the church to repent. If their faith and trust are in Jesus Christ and their confession is that God has raised Him from the dead, they are saved and will be included with all of the saints, both living and dead, in the rapture.

To Sardis: The Church of the Reformation (1517 AD to the Rapture)

1 "And to the angel of the church in Sardis write,

'These things says He who has the seven Spirits of God and the seven stars: "I know your works, that you have a name that you are alive, but you are dead. 2 Be watchful, and strengthen the things which remain, that are ready to die, for I have not found your works perfect before God. 3 Remember therefore how you have received and heard; hold fast and repent. Therefore if you will not watch, I will come upon you as a thief, and you will not know what hour I will come upon you. 4 You have a few names even in Sardis who have not defiled their garments; and they shall walk with Me in white, for they are worthy. 5 He who overcomes shall be clothed in white garments, and I will not blot out his name from the Book of Life; but I will confess his name before My Father and before His angels. 6 He who has an ear, let him hear what the Spirit says to the churches." (Revelation 3:1-6)

Chapter 3 in Revelation begins with the letter to the church in Sardis. As we'll see, this church of Sardis represents the churches of the Reformation, particularly the proliferation of various Protestant denominations we see today. As I mentioned with the last church, the church of Thyatira, that signified the Church of Rome, there are many who may be offended by my comments. This may be especially true since, unlike the church of Thyatira, and despite some very good things

Jesus had to say about Thyatira, this church of Sardis is the first church to receive nothing but condemnation from Jesus.

Sardis is the name of a precious gemstone, typically reddish brown in color, and also the name of this city, likely because the stone was mined in the same area. Sardis was a very large and important city, but despite its wealth and reputation, its era of greatness was in the past. A major earthquake in 17 AD leveled the city as well as much of the western part of Lydia. According to ancient historians, the earthquake was particularly tragic because it struck at night when everyone was sleeping. Sardis was completely rebuilt with funding provided by the Roman emperor, but it would never again live up to its reputation.

Most scholars and church historians who teach that these seven churches represent the entire church age will place the beginning of the time period represented by the church of Sardis in 1517 AD. It was on October 31, 1517, that Martin Luther, a Catholic priest, and an Augustinian friar nailed the Ninety-five theses to the door of the Wittenberg Castle church. This marked the beginning of what is known as the Protestant Reformation. Luther's document supported two foundational beliefs that became the basis of the Reformation. These two central beliefs are that the Bible is the sole authority of Christian doctrine rather than the teachings and traditions of the Church of Rome, and secondly, that we are saved by grace through faith (Ephesians 2:8) and not by our good works and deeds. Truth be told, these two beliefs were stated in the first two of Luther's Ninety-five theses. The others primarily attacked the practice of selling indulgences to the poor and the greed of the Catholic pope in using these indulgences as a way of raising funds for St. Peter's Basilica in Rome.

In verse 2 of chapter 3, Jesus says, ***"I know your works, that you have a name that you are alive, but you are dead."*** The Reformation was a great revival of Christianity. It literally breathed new life into what had become a dead religion for many. It brought the authority and the study of the Bible back to the forefront of church discipline and doctrine. Within a very short time, the Bible was translated into the language of the people. Prior to this successful reformation in 1517 AD, the only authorized Bible was in Latin, which Jerome had translated back in 382 AD. Interestingly, the Bible translation by Jerome was understood to be the "Vulgate," from the Latin *editio vulgate*, meaning "common version." Ideally, the Bible was to be in the common language of the people, something that could be read, appreciated, and put into practice by the people. Within a few hundred years, however, very few could speak or read Latin, and therefore, in practice, as the people could not read Latin and all other translations were prohibited by the church, the Bible took a back seat to church tradition.

But when the Reformation took off, the common people of Europe, not just clergymen, suddenly had the Bible available in their own languages. In addition, the invention of the printing press by Johannes Gutenberg in Germany in the 15th century, just prior to the Reformation, meant that not only the Bible but the teachings of the great reformers like Luther, Calvin, Knox, and others could be easily disseminated to the people. The teachings included what we understand to be the "five solas."

The five solas were used to define the five key teachings of the Reformation. They are:

1. **Sola scriptura**: "Scripture alone"

2. **Sola fide**: "faith alone"

3. **Sola gratia**: "grace alone"

4. **Solo Christo**: "Christ alone"

5. **Soli Deo gloria**: "to the glory of God alone"

As people began to read the Bible, they discovered that while this concept of the five solas was new, the truth had been there all along.

The Bible clearly teaches that people are saved, set free, and forgiven of their sins by grace alone, through faith alone, and through Christ alone. This was the teaching of the Apostle Paul and others. This reformation started off as a revival, and for hundreds of years, it was these churches that came out of the reformation that brought life, grace, and peace through the public pronouncement of the word of God. These are the true works that bring glory to God.

However, Jesus said that the reputation is there, but actually you (the church of Sardis, the mainline denominations that came out of the Reformation) are dead! This decline didn't happen overnight; it took hundreds of years, but many can see that it is quite apparent today. The decline is most visible in the western world, including, perhaps most obviously, the United States. Because of the First Amendment and religious freedom, the United States has the most Protestant denominations and protestants in the world, accounting for roughly half of the population.

Church attendance in the United States likely peaked during World War II and remained high until about twenty years ago. Many studies have observed this trend, which is most pronounced in what we would consider the mainline Protestant churches. This would include Baptists, Presbyterians, Methodists, Lutherans, Episcopalians, the Church of God, and some of their spin-off denominations, often with similar names. Many of these denominations are living off of their reputations but are losing attendees at a remarkable rate. Quite frankly, the more people they lose, the more these denominations drift further and further from the truth that gave birth to the Reformation over five hundred years ago. The problem has been that they have been riding on their reputation, but they have been embracing the craziness of a culture that has been moving away from Biblical truths for the past hundred years.

To these churches (and others), Jesus says, *"Be watchful, and strengthen the things which remain, that are ready to die, for I have not found your works perfect before God. 3 Remember therefore how you have received and heard; hold fast and repent"* (verses 2–3a).

With Jesus, there is always the opportunity to repent! Like in the parable of the prodigal son, the Father is always waiting to receive us back home. The gospel popularized by the Reformation was simple; it was to bring people back to a relationship with God through Jesus Christ.

It is to this church that Jesus says, *"Therefore if you will not watch, I will come upon you as a thief, and you will not know what hour I will come upon you" (verse 3b).*

The second coming of Jesus Christ at the end of this present age is said in the New Testament to *"come like a thief in the night" (1 Thessalonians 5:2).* Jesus uses these words to indicate that this church will be present at the end of the age, at the time of the rapture.

Jesus said,

> **43 "But know this, that if the master of the house had known what hour the thief would come, he would have watched and not allowed his house to be broken into. 44 Therefore you also be ready, for the Son of Man is coming at an hour you do not expect." (Matthew 24:43-44)**

Jesus closes this letter to the church of Sardis with the hope that all is not lost in the church in Sardis. Jesus acknowledges that when He returns, there will be *"a few names even in Sardis who have not defiled their garments" (verse 4),* indicating that these few are not dead but very much alive. *"Not defiled their garments"* is like saying they have not bought into the corruption, the decline in the doctrines, the beliefs, and the practices that this church originally had. The Reformation of the 16th century was a powerful revival, and while many of the mainline traditional churches have nothing left but their reputation, there are at least a few that remain faithful. They will not be caught unaware when the Lord returns, and they are those that look forward to His glorious appearing.

Jesus promises that some will be worthy, and *"He who overcomes shall be clothed in white garments, and I will not blot out his name from the Book of Life; but I will confess his name before My Father and before His angels" (verse 5).* The picture of the saints dressed in white and standing before the Lord in the presence of the Father and the angels is depicted most clearly in Revelation 20:11–15. The promise from God is that if you put your faith solely in Jesus and His finished work on the cross, you are saved. Your name has been written in the book of life, and the promise is that it will not be removed.

To Philadelphia: The Missionary Church (1792 AD to the Rapture)

7 "And to the angel of the church in Philadelphia write, 'These things says He who is holy, He who is true, "He who has the key of David, He who opens and no one shuts, and shuts and no one opens": 8 I know your works. See, I have set before you an open door, and no one can shut it; for you have a little strength, have kept My word, and have not denied My name. 9 Indeed I will make those of the synagogue of Satan, who say they are Jews and are not, but lie—indeed I will make them come and worship before your feet, and to know that I have loved you. 10 Because you have kept My command to persevere, I also will keep you from the hour of trial which shall come upon the whole world, to test those who dwell on the earth. 11 Behold, I am coming quickly! Hold fast what you have, that no one may take your crown.

12 He who overcomes, I will make him a pillar in the temple of My God, and he shall go out no more. And I will write on him the name of My God and the name of the city of My God, the New Jerusalem, which

> *comes down out of heaven from My God. And I will write on him My new name. 13 He who has an ear, let him hear what the Spirit says to the churches." '*
> *(Revelation 3:7-13)*

The sixth of the seven churches in the book of Revelation is the church in Philadelphia. Like the church before it, it represents a more recent church age, possibly beginning in the late 18th century. Unlike the church before it, the church in Philadelphia is fully commended for their works, how they have kept the word of God, and how they have not denied His name. Reading this letter to the church in Philadelphia, we can see that the Lord gives many commendations for this church, with no rebukes or chastisements.

What is it about this church that makes it receive such commendation, and why do we mark the start of this church in the late 19th century? The first clue is the name "Philadelphia," a name that means "brotherly love." Jesus said, *"By this all will know that you are My disciples, if you have love for one another" (John 13:35).* This is a church that is marked by love for one another. We date the beginning of this church from the clue that Jesus gave, *"I have set before you an open door, and no one can shut it" (verse 8).* Often, the open door in the Bible indicates an invitation, and in particular an invitation to share the gospel, particularly as a missionary, and also to do the will of the Lord. In 1 Corinthians 16:9, the Apostle Paul writes that a door has been opened to him to continue to minister in Ephesus. In Acts 14:27, Paul and Barnabas report how God had opened the door of faith to the Gentiles.

Church historians write about the great missionary explosion of the 19th century, which began in many ways with missionary William Carey. William Carey is considered the father of the modern missionary and the forerunner of the missionary movement. Carey was born in 1761 and had a gift for language. By the time he was twenty-four, he was the pastor of a Baptist church in England. In 1792, he published

"An Enquiry into the Obligations of Christians to Use Means for the Conversion of the Heathens," known simply as the *"Enquiry."* The work was based on Carey's observation that the church had lost its missionary focus and passion for the Great Commission that Jesus gave in Matthew.

> **19 "Go therefore and make disciples of all the nations, baptizing them in the name of the Father and of the Son and of the Holy Spirit, 20 teaching them to observe all things that I have commanded you; and lo, I am with you always, even to the end of the age." Amen. (Matthew 28:19-20)**

In this same year of 1792, Carey organized what would become known as the *"Baptist Missionary Society."* The next year, William Carey traveled to Calcutta, India, with his wife and children and began his translation of the Bible into the Bengali language. We will use this date, 1792, as the beginning of this church age, associated with the church in Philadelphia, as William Cary, known as the "father of modern missions," successfully brought the gospel to India and started the Baptist Missionary Society that same year.

The Baptist Missionary Society was the first foreign missionary organization launched following the revival in both Europe and North America known as the **"Great Awakening."** This began a fervent and passionate embrace of foreign missions that continued through the 20th century and to this day.

The missionary church movement that began over two hundred years ago has changed the trajectory of the church dramatically, as the church at the time was very much a European and Western (including North and South American) institution. Today, the church is established and growing in Africa and Asia.

Asian Christianity can be traced back to the Apostle Paul visiting India as early as 52 AD. The great Portuguese explorer, Vasco de Gama, in the early 16th century, was greeted by "Thomas Christians" on the

Malabar Coast of India, and these Thomas Christians considered the Portuguese to be their Christian brothers. One of the highest growth rates of Christians in the 20th and 21st centuries was in China, particularly in the house churches, and today estimates of Christians in China exceed over one hundred million, with over fifty-five million in unregulated and largely underground house churches in what continues to be an officially atheist and communist country.

It is to this passionate, missionary church that Jesus promises safety during the coming time of trial:

> *Because you have kept My command to persevere, I also will keep you from the hour of trial which shall come upon the whole world, to test those who dwell on the earth. 11 Behold, I am coming quickly! Hold fast what you have, that no one may take your crown. (verses 10–11)*

These verses in the third chapter of Revelation to the church in Philadelphia are some of the clearest references to a pre-tribulation rapture of the church. The promise is clearly that the Lord will keep the faithful "*from the hour of trial which shall come upon the whole world, to test those who dwell on the earth*" *(verse 10)*. This "hour of trial" is translated from the Greek word *horas*. Note that this is a very broad trial or tribulation as it impacts the *"whole world."*

Of all of the churches present during the time of the return of Jesus, this church of Philadelphia is a type of the true church, representing the bride of Christ. Jesus returns to the earth for His bride and takes all of the faithful with Him back to His father's house (John 14:1-6). While some commentators and theologians adhere to a "partial rapture" theory, Scripture never makes this distinction. Partial rapture claims that only some Christians will be raptured prior to the beginning of the tribulation, while others will go through the tribulation with all of those who dwell on the earth in order to sift the church and remove the unfaithful. However, Scripture tells us, *"There is therefore now no condemnation to those who are in Christ Jesus, who do not walk according to the flesh, but according to the Spirit" (Romans 8:1),* and nowhere in the Scripture do we see that the church is to suffer the wrath of God. On the contrary, wrath is juxtaposed or contrasted with salvation, specifically in reference to the future of the believer.

> *9 For God did not appoint us to wrath, but to obtain salvation through our Lord Jesus Christ, 10 who died for us, that whether we wake or sleep, we should live together with Him. (1 Thessalonians 5:9-10)*

I do not adhere to a partial rapture theory and believe that the Bible clearly teaches that all believers, all who have been saved by the blood of Jesus Christ, including those that are mature as well as the immature, the obedient as well as those that are disobedient, will be caught up together with all of those that have already died in Christ and will be with the Lord in the event we know as the rapture. The rapture is the fulfillment of the church age. It is the end of the age and precedes the seven years known as the tribulation and the time of Jacob's trial that bring judgment, God's wrath on an unbelieving world, and at the same time, redemption and salvation to the people of Israel.

This church in Philadelphia, representing the missionary church, will be present until the rapture of the church, along with the remnant faithful of the church in Thyatira and the remnant faithful of the church in Sardis. There is one more church to review and understand; it is clearly the modern church and will also be present at the time of the rapture. The question is, "Will any be found faithful?"

To Laodicea: The Lukewarm Church (Present Time to the Rapture)

14 "And to the angel of the church of the Laodiceans write,

'These things says the Amen, the Faithful and True Witness, the Beginning of the creation of God: 15 I know your works, that you are neither cold nor hot. I could wish you were cold or hot. 16 So then, because you are lukewarm, and neither cold nor hot, I will vomit you out of My mouth. 17 Because you say, 'I am rich, have become wealthy, and have need of nothing'—and do not know that you are wretched, miserable, poor, blind, and naked—18 I counsel you to buy from Me gold refined in the fire, that you may be rich; and white garments, that you may be clothed, that the shame of your nakedness may not be revealed; and anoint your eyes with eye salve, that you may see. 19 As many as I love, I rebuke and chasten. Therefore be zealous and repent. 20 Behold, I stand at the door and knock. If anyone hears My voice and opens the door, I will come in to him and dine with him, and he with Me. 21 To him who overcomes I will grant to sit with Me on My throne, as I also overcame and sat down with My Father on His throne. 22 He who has an ear, let him hear what the Spirit says to the churches." ' (Revelation 3:14-22)

As the church in Laodicea is the last of the seven churches, and as we believe that these churches represent the entirety of the church age, then this last church is with us in the present time. Laodicea is often called the "lukewarm church," as Jesus gives this church one of the strongest rebukes: *"So then, because you are lukewarm, and neither cold nor hot, I will vomit you out of My mouth" (verse 16).*

While many commentaries and many theologians date the time period of this church's beginning only recently, perhaps within the past hundred years, it is in fact the lukewarm characteristic of the church that indicates this type of church has always been present. Like the church in Sardis, this church in Laodicea receives only condemnation, rebukes, and chastisements. Jesus has nothing good to say to them. They are urged to repent, to recognize that they are *"wretched, miserable, poor, blind, and naked" (verse 17)*. The most amazing thing we find with this church is that they are so completely unaware of their true spiritual condition. They are in a state of denial, and Jesus calls them to *"be zealous and repent" (verse 19)*.

As we have seen in a couple of the seven churches, this name, Laodicea, is a clue to one of the sources of their problems. The word Laodicea is a combination of two Greek words; the word *laos*, which we have mentioned before, refers to people. It's the same root from which we get the word "laity." This root is also found in the term we discussed earlier in the *Doctrine of the Nicolaitans,* which was associated with the churches of Ephesus and Pergamum. However, the second Greek root in this word, Laodicea, is the word *dike* (Strongs 1349), referring to justice, a ruling, or a decision. Therefore, in this way, Laodicea could be translated as the *"Rule of the People."*

As Jesus is the head of the church, the Laodiceans choose "majority rule," which leads to apostasy. The Apostle Paul wrote in his epistle to the Colossians, *"And He is the head of the body, the church, who is the beginning, the firstborn from the dead, that in all things He may have the preeminence" (Colossians 1:18).* This is just one of over one hundred verses we can quote that identify the unique role that Jesus and the Holy Spirit have in leading, ruling, and guiding the church. In a letter to his apprentice Timothy, the Apostle Paul warned that, in the latter days, there would be a time when people would stop listening to the truth and be taught by false teachers.

3 For the time will come when they will not endure sound doctrine, but according to their own desires, because they have itching ears, they will heap up for themselves teachers; 4 and they will turn their ears away from the truth, and be turned aside to fables. (2 Timothy 4:3-4)

This end time, modern, lukewarm church seems to be *"rich, have become wealthy, and have need of nothing" (verse 17).* The ancient city of Laodicea was a wealthy commercial center. Historians tell us that this inland city had a famous medical school known for a particular eye salve. In addition, as they were inland, there was a Roman aqueduct that brought fresh water from the nearby mountains, but by the time it reached the city, the water was lukewarm.

Jesus uses these particular details to show them how much they need to repent and come back to Him. He refers to the lukewarm water as their faith, which was lukewarm. He advises them to purchase *"eye salve, that you may see" (verse 18).*

A pastor friend of mine pointed out that Jesus introduces Himself to this church as *"the Amen, the Faithful and True Witness, the Beginning of the creation of God," (verse 14)* and told me to key on the words, *"creation of God."* He explained that it is interesting to note that in the past 2,000 years since Pentecost, it was only recently that the people in the church needed to be reminded that the source of God's creation is in fact Jesus Christ. It's only recently that the theory of a "big bang," said to have occurred roughly 13.8 billion years ago, and the theory of evolution have replaced the Biblical account of creation clearly taught in the book of Genesis.

Jesus, however, has some good news not only for the people of this church age but for anyone, as He says, *"Behold, I stand at the door and knock. If anyone hears My voice and opens the door, I will come in to him and dine with him, and he with Me" (verse 20).*

This is a general invitation to anyone and everyone. Each of us, regardless of our church background, our denomination, or the bogus teaching we may or may not have heard, has the opportunity to personally invite Jesus into our lives. Perhaps you have seen the popular paintings and illustrations of Jesus standing at the door. If you notice, you'll see that the artists don't include a handle on the outside, where Jesus is standing, indicating that you are the one who needs to open the door.

As we close out our review of all seven churches, it's wonderful to note that Jesus has made this promise in the picture of Him knocking at the door of our hearts. Throughout the entirety of the church age, each individual that comes to faith in Jesus Christ as Lord and Savior comes the same way: by openly declaring that Jesus is Lord and by believing that God has raised Him from the dead (Romans 10:9).

CHAPTER TEN
BIRTH PAINS

Jesus made it clear that no one will actually know the day or the hour of His coming. However, at the same time, Jesus did answer the question posed to Him by His Apostles about the timing of His second coming.

> *4 And Jesus answered and said to them: "Take heed that no one deceives you. 5 For many will come in My name, saying, 'I am the Christ,' and will deceive many. 6 And you will hear of wars and rumors of wars. See that you are not troubled; for all these things must come to pass, but the end is not yet. 7 For nation will rise against nation, and kingdom against kingdom. And there will be famines, pestilences, and earthquakes in various places. 8 All these are the beginning of sorrows."*

> *(Matthew 24:4-8)*

The best source for clues regarding the timing of the second coming, also called the second advent of Jesus Christ, is in what is referred to as the Olivet Discourse or Olivet Prophecy, and specifically Matthew chapter 24, where Jesus responds to the Apostles' very important question. In fact, it is the same question that Christians are asking today.

"Tell us, when will these things be? And what will be the sign of Your coming, and of the end of the age?" (Matthew 24:3)

We covered the first two verses of Matthew 24 in our chapter 3 when we discussed Jesus' prophecy about the destruction of the temple. There is, however, much that Jesus has to say in response to the question that the Apostles asked. He had told them, *"Assuredly, I say to you, not one stone shall be left here upon another, that shall not be thrown down" (Matthew 24:2b).* Scripture tells us that Jesus and the Apostles then walked from the temple mount to the Mount of Olives.

Today, visitors to historic Jerusalem can travel from the temple mount to the Mount of Olives by walking through the Lions' Gate, also called St. Stephen's Gate, through the Kidron Valley, and up again to the Mount of Olives. The journey takes about fifteen minutes. This area is so rich in history and also plays an important role in end time prophecy.

Jesus had entered Jerusalem on Palm Sunday by traveling from the Mount of Olives through the descent into the Kidron valley. He entered the old city through the Eastern Gate, riding on a donkey in fulfillment of Scripture (Zechariah 9:9). Visitors to the old city of Jerusalem today will take note that this Eastern Gate, referred to as the "Beautiful Gate" in Scripture (Acts 3:2), is now called the "Golden Gate," and it is closed and completely walled up. It was closed in 1540 AD with brick and mortar and large stones that actually restored a portion of the old city wall. The Eastern Gate was sealed up by order of Sultan Suleiman the Magnificent, the ruler of the Ottoman Empire. He did this so that the Jewish Messiah could not pass through the eastern gate, in fulfillment of Jewish tradition that was loosely based on Scripture. In addition to the sealed-up gate, to ensure that the Jewish Messiah would not enter the city through the eastern gate, Sultan Suleiman the Magnificent also had a cemetery added just below the old city gate, trusting that religious Jews would be prohibited from passing through a cemetery.

Getting back to our Scripture referenced earlier, the Apostles had asked Jesus important questions about the sign of His coming and the end of the age. These verses are so important that they are worth repeating:

> *4 "Take heed that no one deceives you. 5 For many will come in My name, saying, 'I am the Christ,' and will deceive many. 6 And you will hear of wars and rumors of wars. See that you are not troubled; for all these things must come to pass, but the end is not yet. 7 For nation will rise against nation, and kingdom against kingdom. And there will be famines, pestilences, and earthquakes in various places. 8 All these are the beginning of sorrows" (Matthew 24:4-8)*

There has likely been more conversation regarding the last days referencing these four verses than any other passage in the Bible. Who hasn't heard about wars, rumors of wars, famines, and earthquakes all pointing to the end of the age? However, this is not what Jesus said. Jesus is making a statement regarding those things throughout history that, while unfortunate and often devastating, are not necessarily a sign of His coming and the end of the age.

Jesus tells us that there must be false messiahs who deceive many, as well as wars and reports (rumors) of wars. They must happen because they are part of man's fallen nature. They have been going on for thousands of years and will continue until the end. Jesus said, *"All these things must come to pass, but the end is not yet" (verse 6).*

Jesus continues and says that *"nation will rise against nation" (verse 7).* The word "nation" in this context refers to the Greek word *"éthnos,"* from which we get the English word "ethnicity," and thus does not necessarily refer to countries rising up against other countries, but to people groups rising up against other people groups. This, along with **"*famines and earthquakes from place to place*" (*verse 7*),** marks what Jesus calls the beginning of labor pains, also known as birth pains.

Most people know about birth pains, and as a man, I have been told I cannot possibly fully understand how intense birth pains actually get as a woman's pregnancy is drawing to a close! However, for the purpose of illustration, allow me to elaborate.

While life begins at conception, it is not uncommon for a woman to take a pregnancy test to determine whether or not she is carrying a baby. Months go by, and little by little, there are telltale signs that confirm that there is a baby coming. The doctor checks periodically to make sure the baby and the mother are doing well, and one of the things the doctor will tell the mother about is "birth pains." These birth pains, the doctor explains, are the final signs that the baby is about to be delivered, so the doctor explains how they are different from other pains and contractions she may experience.

From the moment of conception, there was a feeling, an assurance, and a certainty that a baby was on the way. Just before the baby is born, the mother and father began to prepare for the day they would finally see their child face-to-face. However, during most of the pregnancy, life went on as usual. No doubt the last trimester, unlike the first six months, was somewhat challenging for the mother. Occasionally, especially during the third and final trimester, the mother feels contractions and thinks, "This must be it," only to discover that it isn't! This is why the doctor has already told her about Braxton Hicks contractions, named after a British doctor named John Braxton Hicks.

While these Braxton Hicks contractions are very similar to the real thing, they are not. The biggest difference is that with true birth pains, the pains begin relatively mildly and are initially spaced a long time apart. However, the one thing that all true birth pains have in common is that they continually get more intense and more frequent. Ultimately, a baby is born; there is absolutely no doubt about it, and that which was only known through intense pain suddenly becomes the greatest joy in the birth of the baby.

This is exactly what Jesus meant when he said that these preliminary signs are like birth pains. They are the final act in the natural order of things. They begin relatively mildly but quickly gain intensity, frequency, and duration.

Many believe that while all of the naturally occurring, unfortunate, and often devastating events that Jesus mentioned are in themselves not necessarily a sign of His return, these devastating events are to become more intense and more frequent.

Few can argue that what we have seen in the past few years is anything but normal. Most of us only have our own community or perhaps our nation as a reference point, but what we have seen in one country, the United States, Canada, Israel, Great Britain, Australia, etc., is happening in nearly every country in the world.

And it's not just one "pain," it's an amazing number of "pains," all happening at the same time, with all of the governments of the world implementing severe and often draconian measures. Here in the United States, we have not only had the lockdowns, the business closures, and the mandates associated with COVID-19, but we have also had seasons of political unrest. *Black Lives Matter, Antifa, Critical Race Theory, LGBTQ,* and climate change activists have all had their opportunities to advance their radical agendas beyond what seemed possible just a few years ago. What previously was a conspiracy theory has become a regular talking point for organizations like the United Nations and the World Economic Forum. These talking points include a *new world order, a great reset, and a global call to end borders and nationalism.*

Regardless of whether economic decline, climate change, the Corona virus, crime, or CRT are in themselves true crises or have been manufactured for maximum political capital, the result is the same. No one escapes these pains, which are becoming more intense and more frequent. They all point to one thing: these are the birth pains that Jesus referred to as a sign of the end of the age and of His second coming.

Do Not Be Deceived

Before we move on from Jesus' comments to His disciples on the Mount of Olives, we need to go back to one of the greatest warnings that Jesus mentioned, and His words, *"Take heed that no one deceives you" (verse 4).*

This comment about deception is the very first thing that Jesus wanted His disciples, His followers, to know. He warns His disciples, and by extension, all of us, as we begin to see these signs, not to be deceived.

One of the hardest things for the believer living in the period just prior to the coming tribulation and second coming will be dealing with deception. I do not believe it is a coincidence at all that everyone has heard the term "fake news," and it's often applied to both sides of the political divide, those supporting a cause or a government action, or science experts, and those opposing the same.

Deception is rampant today, which is indeed one of the signs that we are truly nearing the end of the age and quickly approaching His second coming. For the believer, Jesus gives us some hope that we will not be deceived and says,

> *"For false christs and false prophets will rise and show great signs and wonders to deceive, if possible, even the elect." (Matthew 24:24)*

This verse is referring to the believers that are still present during the actual tribulation and specifically to the wonders these false prophets perform. This protection, and this promise, however, most likely include all believers living during the period of deception preceding the tribulation. In either case, we should be praying and reading the Bible. Believers through all generations need to be prepared for the Lord's return at any time.

Are You Ready?

To be prepared for the Lord to return at any time means that you are ready. The question is especially important considering that we have already seen what many would describe as "birth pains," meaning that we are closer today than ever before to the Day of the Lord.

CHAPTER ELEVEN

THE DAY OF THE LORD

T he "Day of the Lord" is likely one of the more commonly used phrases referring to some future time of judgment associated with the coming of the Lord or the judgment of God. It is also one of the more commonly misunderstood phrases that is used by scholars, pastors, teachers, and others.

The concept of a day in the Bible is similar to our common use of the word in that it can mean both an actual 24-hour day or some part of those 24 hours, and it can also mean a span of time. For example, it is not uncommon for someone to say, "I can't wait for that day!" when referring to something positive, such as, "I can't wait for that day when I finally retire!" It can also be something that is unlikely, such as "That will be the day," referring to when a debt is repaid, or a person wins the lottery.

In the Bible, the "Day of the Lord" is referenced over twenty times and typically refers to the specific period of time when God brings judgment and His wrath. In both the Old Testament and the New Testament, it is described as a *"day of darkness" (Amos 5:8)*, a *"day of dark clouds, a time appointed for the nations" (Ezekiel 30:3)*, *"as destruction from the Almighty" (Isaiah 13:6)*, like *"destruction from the Almighty" (Joel 1:15)*, and a *"day of vengeance" (Isaiah 34:8)*.

One of the more familiar verses that references the Day of the Lord is from the New Testament, where Paul says, *"For you yourselves know perfectly that the day of the Lord so comes as a thief in the night"* (1 *Thessalonians 5:2).*

I mentioned before that I believe that this phrase, "the Day of the Lord," is one of the more commonly misunderstood phrases as well. The primary reason is a failure to take the Bible's prophecies literally. As I write these words, I realize I have mentioned the need to take prophecy literally rather than "symbolically" a number of times already in these first ten chapters, and no doubt I'll mention it again in the chapters to come.

Let me give a quick example that helps explain both the need to take prophecy literally as well as a segue into our conversation on the Day of the Lord. At Christmas, we often hear the Scripture from the Gospel of Luke, where the Angel Gabriel comes to the Virgin Mary. The dialogue I want to call your attention to begins in verse 30.

> *30 Then the angel said to her, "Do not be afraid, Mary, for you have found favor with God. 31 And behold, you will conceive in your womb and bring forth a Son, and shall call His name Jesus. 32 He will be great, and will be called the Son of the Highest; and the Lord God will give Him the throne of His father David. 33 And He will reign over the house of Jacob forever, and of His kingdom there will be no end." (Luke 1:30-33)*

As Christians, we embrace these verses and the narrative of the virgin birth of Jesus as part of our faith and as part of our understanding of the Scriptures. Have you noticed, however, that what the Angel Gabriel told Mary was prophetic? As it is a prophecy, we want to take it literally whenever possible, and we see that there are seven parts to this prophecy. Five were fulfilled in the first coming of Jesus, and they were fulfilled literally:

1) *You will conceive*

2) *You will bring forth a son*

3) *You shall call His name Jesus*

4) *He will be great*

5) *He will be called Son of the Highest*

And here is the lesson we all should learn: The next two things that the Angel Gabriel says to the Virgin Mary are also prophetic. Just as the first five prophetic statements the angel made were fulfilled literally, so shall the remaining two.

6) *The Lord God will give Him the throne of His father David*

7) *He will reign over the house of Jacob (Israel) forever*

When will these two prophetic pronouncements to Mary about her son be fulfilled? They will be fulfilled on the Day of the Lord! This is exactly how we are to interpret the twenty direct references to the Day of the Lord and over two thousand references in the Old and New Testaments to the same time period. One of my favorite Bible teachers is David Jeremiah, of Turning Point Radio and Television Ministries and senior pastor of Shadow Mountain Community Church. Allow me to borrow him for just a minute. Dr. Jeremiah has said that scholars have identified 1845 references alone to the second coming. The Day of the Lord cannot be understood apart from the second coming of Jesus.

One of the other ways that the Bible, through the prophets, has referred to this time at the end is by using the words "last days," including variations of the same, including last day, latter days, and those days. Here are some examples. Notice again the overriding theme of judgment, calamity, and disaster.

"Look, I am making known to you what shall happen in the latter time of the indignation; for at the appointed time the end shall be." (Daniel 8:19)

"Afterward the children of Israel shall return and seek the Lord their God and David their king. They shall fear the Lord and His goodness in the latter days." (Hosea 3:5)

"Your gold and silver are corroded, and their corrosion will be a witness against you and will eat your flesh like fire. You have heaped up treasure in the last days." (James 5:3)

"You will come up against My people Israel like a cloud, to cover the land. It will be in the latter days that I will bring you against My land, so that the nations may know Me, when I am hallowed in you, O Gog, before their eyes." (Ezekiel 38:16)

These are just a few of the many references to the last days, which always include the second coming of the Lord, also known as the Day of the Lord. As we said earlier, the Day of the Lord also describes a period of time, and many scholars understand this specific time to be the seven years of the tribulation, also known as "Daniel's seventh week" (Daniel 9:24) and the "Time of Jacob's Trouble" (Jeremiah 30:7).

You may be thinking, "Wait a minute, this is too much information to understand!" I agree completely; however, just like any other teaching in the Scriptures, the Bible will interpret the Bible, and this is why we have already laid out ten chapters regarding the end times and have a number of chapters still to go. So just keep reading!

The Apostle Paul refers to this Day of the Lord as the blessed hope for those who fully trust in God's grace through faith in Jesus Christ.

11 "For the grace of God that brings salvation has appeared to all men, 12 teaching us that, denying ungodliness and worldly lusts, we should live soberly, righteously, and godly in the present age, 13 looking for the blessed hope and glorious appearing of our great God and Savior Jesus Christ, 14 who gave Himself for us, that He might redeem us from every lawless deed and purify for Himself His own special people, zealous for good works." (Titus 2:11-14)

Don't miss those words in verse 13: "blessed hope." If I told you that you were to receive a blessing, would you hope for something good or something bad? This is not a rhetorical question, as I want you to say to yourself that the blessed hope, the appearing of our great God and savior Jesus Christ, is good, very good!

In this way, we understand that, while the Day of the Lord includes the time of tribulation, the time of judgment, and the time of vengeance for a period of seven years, the believer who is taken in the rapture of the church at some point immediately prior to the tribulation period is encouraged, strengthened, and blessed.

Many know John 3:16, but we also need to embrace the next verse if we are to understand this blessed hope.

17 "For God did not send His Son into the world to condemn the world, but that the world through Him might be saved. 18 "He who believes in Him is not condemned; but he who does not believe is condemned already, because he has not believed in the name of the only begotten Son of God." (John 3:17-18).

When the Lord returns, He will first gather His own and transport them into heaven and to His Father's house. For those who have rejected the opportunity to know the love of God that is uniquely expressed in the offer of forgiveness through Jesus Christ, the Day of the Lord will be a fearful time of judgment, calamity, and retribution. While the Scriptures speak of multitudes that will be saved during the tribulation, the emphasis appears to be on those who are the descendants of Abraham, what we know as the people of Israel.

Let's turn our attention to what the Apostle Paul revealed about the Day of the Lord. We can understand much about the second coming of Jesus Christ because of the teachings and writings of the Apostle Paul. In both 1 and 2 Thessalonians, the Apostle Paul speaks directly to the times and seasons associated with the coming Day of the Lord. For example:

> *1 But concerning the times and the seasons, brethren, you have no need that I should write to you. 2 For you yourselves know perfectly that the day of the Lord so comes as a thief in the night. 3 For when they say, "Peace and safety!" then sudden destruction comes upon them, as labor pains upon a pregnant woman. And they shall not escape. 4 But you, brethren, are not in darkness, so that this Day should overtake you as a thief. 5 You are all sons of light and sons of the day. We are not of the night nor of darkness. 6 Therefore let us not sleep, as others do, but let us watch and be sober. 7 For those who sleep, sleep at night, and those who get drunk are drunk at night. 8 But let us who are of the day be sober, putting on the breastplate of faith and love, and as a helmet the hope of salvation. 9 For God did not appoint us to wrath, but to obtain salvation through our Lord Jesus Christ, 10 who died for us, that whether we wake or sleep, we should live together with Him.*

*11 Therefore comfort each other and edify one another,
just as you also are doing.(1 Thessalonians 5:1-11)*

Paul starts off this passage by saying, *"concerning the times and the seasons" (verse 1)*. He doesn't define these times and seasons, as he explains, *"For you yourselves know perfectly" (verse 2)*. Paul says that they already know it; it's already part of what he has taught them previously; he has been with them in the past, and the Apostle Paul refers to the coming "Day of the Lord."

The Apostle Paul's journey to Thessalonica is documented in Acts 17, and we can read and discover that he spent three weeks with them, perhaps a little longer. He's writing to the church that he founded; he is writing to people he knows; he is writing to the leaders of the church that he assigned, appointed, he laid his hands on them, and commissioned them to lead. As he brought the gospel to them just weeks prior, these leaders were all very young in the Lord, mere babes, and still needed further instruction by Paul.

In the few weeks that Paul was with these Thessalonians, these new believers, Paul took the little time that he had, this precious time, and taught the Thessalonians about the return of Jesus and other prophetic matters. Paul taught them about the times and the seasons regarding the return of Jesus. He taught them about the rapture, the coming judgments, and the glorious return of Jesus, even though they were still relatively new believers. This is a good lesson for us. I've noticed that many churches today that do a good job of welcoming new people and introducing them to Jesus do a poor job or no job at all regarding prophecy and teaching them about the second coming. This is unfortunate because prophecy makes up more than 25% of the Bible, and there are eight verses regarding the second coming of Jesus for every one verse that speaks of His first coming. The Apostle Paul would most likely be disappointed that many people today have been taught very little about the Day of the Lord, and that sermons on this and other passages concerning the second coming are rare to nonexistent in many of our churches.

Fortunately, there are still many faithful pastors and churches that teach what we call the "full counsel of the Lord." Earlier, I mentioned one of my favorite Bible teachers, Dr. David Jeremiah, senior pastor of Shadow Mountain Community Church. Allow me to quote him for just a minute.

> *People are often surprised to learn that references to the Second Coming outnumber references to the first coming by a factor of eight to one. Scholars have identified 1,845 different Biblical references to the Second Coming of Jesus Christ. In the Old Testament, Christ's return is emphasized in no less than 17 books and the New Testament authors speak of it in 23 of the 27 books. Seven out of 10 chapters in the New Testament mention His return. In other words, 1 out of every 30 verses in the New Testament teaches us that Jesus Christ is coming back to this earth.*

> **Dr. Jeremiah continues**…*It is predicted throughout the Bible wherever you look. In fact, it's even in the book of Genesis. The Bible says in Hebrews 9:28, "To those who eagerly wait for Him He will appear a second time, apart from sin, for salvation," and it actually begins in the book of Genesis. Did you know that Enoch predicted the Second Coming of Christ? Jude tells us this in Jude 1:14-15. Here's what it says: "Now Enoch, the seventh from Adam, prophesied about these men also, saying, 'Behold, the Lord comes with ten thousands of His saints, to execute judgment on all, to convict all who are ungodly among them of all their ungodly deeds which they have committed.*

(Reference: www.davidjeremiah.org/age-of-signs/5-facts-about-the-second-coming-of-christ)

So, let's return to Paul's teaching. Notice that Paul is reminding the people about what they already know. I appreciate that Paul is not hesitant to go back and teach those things again. As a pastor, I know that people (including myself) need to be reminded often of some of the primary truths of the Bible.

Paul, however, doesn't hold back; he jumps right in, as he wants these believers to be ready.

> *1 Concerning times and seasons, brothers, you have no need for anything to be written to you. 2 For you yourselves know very well that the day of the Lord will come like a thief at night. (verses 1–2)*

Paul says that really there is no need to write to them about this, but then he writes to them about this topic. This is similar to a person who introduces a speaker and says that the person is so famous that he really needs no introduction but then goes on and provides a well-scripted introduction.

The Apostle Paul is reminding these Thessalonian believers of what he had taught them previously. This teaching is so critically important to Paul that he wants to remind them, teach them again, and give them more illustrations and information so that they are fully grounded in it.

Being fully grounded in this teaching includes understanding the profound truths of the church's rapture. It was just in the previous chapter, chapter 4 of 1 Thessalonians, that Paul spoke to them about their relatives, their mothers, fathers, and friends that had died, and he wanted to encourage them. He tells them:

> *13 But I do not want you to be ignorant, brethren, concerning those who have fallen asleep, lest you sorrow*

as others who have no hope. 14 For if we believe that Jesus died and rose again, even so God will bring with Him those who sleep in Jesus.

15 For this we say to you by the word of the Lord, that we who are alive and remain until the coming of the Lord will by no means precede those who are asleep. 16 For the Lord Himself will descend from heaven with a shout, with the voice of an archangel, and with the trumpet of God. And the dead in Christ will rise first. 17 Then we who are alive and remain shall be caught up together with them in the clouds to meet the Lord in the air. And thus we shall always be with the Lord. 18 Therefore comfort one another with these words.

(1 Thessalonians 4:13-18)

Paul is teaching them about the resurrection of the believers, the bride of Christ, which is known as the rapture of the church, and Paul is encouraging them even while talking about those that have died. He speaks of death as "sleep," so those who have died in Christ have fallen asleep in Him. He isn't teaching the false doctrine of "soul sleep" that is embraced by the Jehovah's Witnesses, who use the Scriptures incorrectly and take things out of context. The appropriate context here is physical death and physical resurrection, and Paul is telling them that just as Jesus died and then rose, so will all who die in Jesus be resurrected and come back to life with a new body, a resurrected body.

This is encouraging language that Paul is using. He says "sleep," similar to the language we often use today for death and dying. Jesus said of his friend Lazarus, *"Our friend Lazarus sleeps, but I go that I may wake him up" (John 11:11).*

Paul is encouraging these Thessalonians, and notice at the end of the chapter that Paul says, ***"Therefore comfort one another with these words" (verse 18).***

Paul says this as well in chapter 5, the section of Scripture we were looking at earlier in this section. In verse 11, he says, ***"Therefore comfort each other and edify one another, just as you also are doing."***

These words "console" and "encourage" are similar to the concept that the Day of the Lord is the "blessed hope."

So we understand that what Paul is teaching the Thessalonians, and by extension, what he is teaching us, is critically important. Paul doesn't want us to be ignorant; he wants to remind us of what has already been taught, and Paul says that what he is teaching is actually encouraging; we can take comfort and encourage each other in this teaching.

And that is a good place to start because what Paul is talking about regarding the "times and seasons" and the "Day of the Lord" is God's judgment.

People don't like to think about judgment. We've learned in business that people despise performance reviews, which is why many companies have abandoned annual performance reviews in favor of encouraging periodic coaching. I have found that people also hate coaching if you are in any way critical of their performance.

But God has given us performance standards. We all know the Ten Commandments. We may not all know each of the Ten Commandments, but we would recognize them if we heard them: Don't take the Lord's name in vain; don't steal; don't commit adultery; don't lie; and don't covet. These commandments, according to Jesus, can be summed up as follows: ***"You shall love the Lord your God with all your heart, with all your soul, with all your mind, and with all your strength."*** And then Jesus continues: ***"The second, like it, is this: 'You shall love your neighbor as yourself.' There is no other commandment greater than these" (Mark 12:30-31).***

And this is our performance objective; this is the law of God that we live by, it's the law that is hopefully engraved on our hearts; it's what motivates us and guides us. This is actually what it means to be ready for the Day of the Lord. Because we know God through the power of the Holy Spirit and Jesus Christ, we repent of all of our sins and are guided by these two commands that Jesus gave us, to love God and to love our neighbor.

And while Paul is encouraging us, at the same time he is reminding us that the Day of the Lord will come when many are sleeping, when they are confident that everything is going along fine, when they say "peace and safety," and then face sudden destruction.

Paul is telling those of us who know God, those who are His at His coming, that we will not be overtaken like a thief in the night. Paul tells us we are **"sons of light and sons of the day" (verse 5),** we are to **"watch and be sober" (verse 6),** and that **"God did not appoint us to wrath" (verse 9).**

Why has God delayed His coming?

One of the questions I get often as I'm teaching on the Day of the Lord and the end times is, "Why has Jesus not returned?"

It's a fair question, as it has been nearly 2,000 years since Jesus ascended into heaven and told His disciples that He would return. The return of Jesus Christ is a common topic in the New Testament, and it's obvious from even a casual reading of the Scriptures that the Apostles and the early saints all eagerly anticipated the Lord's coming.

The Apostle Peter gives us one of the reasons in his second epistle.

> *3 Knowing this first: that scoffers will come in the last days, walking according to their own lusts, 4 and saying, "Where is the promise of His coming? For since the fathers fell asleep, all things continue as they were from the beginning of creation." 5 For this they willfully forget: that by the word of God the heavens were of old, and the earth standing out of water and in the*

water, 6 by which the world that then existed perished, being flooded with water. 7 But the heavens and the earth which are now preserved by the same word, are reserved for fire until the day of judgment and perdition of ungodly men.

8 But, beloved, do not forget this one thing, that with the Lord one day is as a thousand years, and a thousand years as one day. 9 The Lord is not slack concerning His promise, as some count slackness, but is longsuffering toward us, not willing that any should perish but that all should come to repentance. (2 Peter 3:3-9)

Often, the Scriptures speak of how God is patient and merciful. The Scriptures tell us He is *"longsuffering and abundant in mercy, forgiving iniquity and transgression"* (Numbers 14:18 also Exodus 34:6, Nehemiah 9:17, Psalm 86:15, Psalm 145:8, etc.).

At the same time, most people understand the need for judgment. We see it in our court systems, and lawyers that argue for both the defendant and the plaintiff in our courts know that the people demand justice. They know that juries, when presented with a crime, any injustice, the loss of a human life, or criminal conduct, whether it is larceny, assault, robbery, or extortion, want to punish because, to them and to us as well, punishment means justice.

We look to the return of the Lord primarily to be with Him, to enter the heavenly realm, to cease from our labor, to be reunited with our loved ones, and to experience the peace that passes all understanding.

As we approach that day, that time of the return of the Lord, we are encouraged by the Lord to be holy. I recently taught my church the concept of holiness and described holiness as "expressing the character and calling of God."

Remember the Apostle Paul's words: "*But you, brethren, are not in darkness, so that this Day should overtake you as a thief. 5 You are all sons of light and sons of the day. We are not of the night nor of darkness"* *(Thessalonians 5:4–5)*. Paul is simply telling the Thessalonian Christians who they are. God has made us sons of the light and sons of the day. This is the work of God; we have to rest in it.

There are, however, those of whom Paul says, *"the day of the Lord so comes as a thief in the night"* *(1 Thessalonians 5:2)*. There are those that have no consideration for the laws of God; there are those that have no knowledge of the Son of God because they suppress the truth. In Romans, Paul says that it is self-evident. He keeps talking about those who are in denial, about those who are in the dark: *"For those who sleep, sleep at night, and those who get drunk are drunk at night"* *(1 Thessalonians 5:7)*.

My mama always told me nothing good happens at night, and while I didn't know it, she was using the same metaphor as the Apostle Paul. The night can be evil, but only because evil people are operating in the darkness.

The Apostle Paul continues: *"But let us who are of the day be sober"* *(1 Thessalonians 5:8a)*. Being sober simply means being serious, doing something intentionally, and weighing the advantages and disadvantages of our actions. The Bible says that sin is pleasurable for a season.

Paul gives us some encouragement and some positive action as he encourages us: *"Putting on the breastplate of faith and love, and as a helmet the hope of salvation"* *(1 Thessalonians 5:8)*. Paul used the image of a soldier's armor to illustrate the idea of watchfulness. If we compare this to the spiritual armor that Paul speaks of in Ephesians 6, there is not an exact correlation. This tells us that Paul saw the idea of spiritual armor as something helpful, a great symbol of how to live a holy and practical life.

Let me conclude this chapter with an extremely important point, and the reason why the Lord's Day is a source of encouragement, the blessed hope:

9 For God did not appoint us to wrath, but to obtain salvation through our Lord Jesus Christ, 10 who died for us, that whether we wake or sleep, we should live together with Him. 11 Therefore comfort each other and edify one another, just as you also are doing.(1 Thessalonians 5:9–11)

The Scriptures tell us that *"there is therefore now no condemnation to those who are in Christ Jesus, who do not walk according to the flesh, but according to the Spirit" (Romans 8:1).* This includes the time described in the Scriptures as the Day of the Lord, the tribulation, the end times, and the time of Jacob's trial. The Scriptures tell us, and the doctrine of the rapture of the church assures us, that those who are His at His coming are the beneficiaries of God's grace and mercy, not His wrath. It is by grace that we are saved through faith; it is a gift of God, not by works. Because we are saved and we belong to Him, we have the ability to call God our father because we have become His adopted sons.

And at the same time, God's mercy is in operation. Mercy can be defined as not receiving the things that we actually deserve. God's mercy is available to everyone! A day of judgment is coming for those who reject Jesus' offer of salvation, for those who mock those who follow Jesus, and for those who mock God's mercy and longsuffering. The Scriptures tell us that God is not willing to have any perish, so He has been withholding judgment until the Day of the Lord.

Be encouraged! I hope that this chapter on the Day of the Lord is encouraging. This Day of the Lord must come. It is the time of Jacob's trial. It is a day of judgment, but it is also a time of redemption. We who are saved are those who have made Jesus the Lord of our lives. We are those whose sins have been forgiven and who have been washed clean by the blood of the lamb. As a result, we do not need to fear the wrath of God, for we have already been redeemed.

The letter from Jesus to the church in Philadelphia should remove all doubt. Jesus says, *"Because you have kept My command to persevere,*

I also will keep you from the hour of trial which shall come upon the whole world, to test those who dwell on the earth" (Revelation 3:10).

Before the destruction of Sodom and Gomorrah, Abraham asked the Lord the question, **"Would You also destroy the righteous with the wicked?" (Genesis 18:23)** God's answer then was "no," as God removed Lot and two of his daughters from the fiery end of those cities.

The Day of the Lord is coming! We see the signs; we see Israel in the land, and we see the nations aligning according to the prophecies of the end times. The only thing you need to do to prepare is to make sure you are right with the Lord. In our own might, we can never be right; we cannot be holy; we cannot be righteous; and we cannot be good enough to merit heaven. But Jesus paid the price for our sins and the sin of the world. His offer of salvation, of redemption, and of eternal life is for whoever will call upon the name of the Lord!

Paul wrote in the tenth chapter of the book of Romans:

> *9 If you confess with your mouth the Lord Jesus and believe in your heart that God has raised Him from the dead, you will be saved. 10 For with the heart one believes unto righteousness, and with the mouth confession is made unto salvation. (Romans 10:9–10)*

CHAPTER TWELVE

THE FOUR HORSEMEN

O ne of the phrases people often know regarding the tribulation or end times is "The Four Horsemen." These four horsemen in the Bible refer to the first four riders on horses that we see in chapter 6 of the book of Revelation with the opening of seven seals.

Interestingly, the four horsemen were popularized 100 years ago as four football players from Notre Dame, under the leadership of legendary coach Knute Rockne. Quarterback Harry Stuhldreher, left halfback Jim Crowley, right halfback Don Miller, and fullback Elmer Layden were part of Notre Dame's extraordinary offensive backfield that won the college national championship in 1924. The sportswriter who coined the term "Four Horsemen" for these four football players from Notre Dame knew his Bible because he stated that their aliases were *famine, pestilence, destruction, and death.*

These four horsemen were popularized not only in the days of Knute Rockne but more recently in 1986. The WWF (an abbreviation for the World Wrestling Federation that changed its name to the World Wrestling Entertainment in 2002) named their top wrestlers The Four Horsemen. The people at the WWF likely didn't understand prophecy but somehow knew that these four horsemen were bad dudes. Interestingly, there were fifteen wrestlers who were part of "The Four Horsemen." But if the Big Ten can have fourteen teams, it shouldn't be surprising to see fifteen "four horsemen."

So, let's depart from professional and college sports and begin to dig into what the Bible has to say about these four horsemen.

These four horsemen are represented in the first four seals that are opened in the sixth chapter of Revelation. These seals that are opened mark the beginning of the tribulation period, the time immediately preceding the second coming of Jesus to the earth. Jesus spoke very clearly of both the tribulation period and his second coming. As we read what Jesus had to say, we'll see there is a strong correlation between these first six seals in the book of Revelation and what Jesus refers to in Matthew 24 as the "birth pangs" at the beginning of the tribulation.

Just prior to His death on Calvary, Jesus points to the temple and says, *"Do you not see all these things? Assuredly, I say to you, not one stone shall be left here upon another, that shall not be thrown down" (Matthew 24:2).* Then a little later, as Jesus was sitting on the Mount of Olives, the disciples came to Him privately, saying,

> *"Tell us, when will these things be? And what will be the sign of Your coming, and of the end of the age?" 4 And Jesus answered and said to them: "Take heed that no one deceives you. 5 For many will come in My name, saying, 'I am the Christ,' and will deceive many. 6 And you will hear of wars and rumors of wars. See that you are not troubled; for all these things must come to pass, but the end is not yet. 7 For nation will rise against nation, and kingdom against kingdom. And there will be famines, pestilences, and earthquakes in various places. 8 All these are the beginning of sorrows."*
> *(Matthew 24:3b-8)*

Many have noticed the correlation in Matthew 24 between these events and the sequence of events in the opening of the seals. Here's what John saw in the opening of the first four seals that he then wrote about in Revelation chapter 6:

First Seal: The Conqueror

1 Now I saw when the Lamb opened one of the seals; and I heard one of the four living creatures saying with a voice like thunder, "Come and see." 2 And I looked, and behold, a white horse. He who sat on it had a bow; and a crown was given to him, and he went out conquering and to conquer.

Second Seal: Conflict on Earth

3 When He opened the second seal, I heard the second living creature saying, "Come and see." 4 Another horse, fiery red, went out. And it was granted to the one who sat on it to take peace from the earth, and that people should kill one another; and there was given to him a great sword.

Third Seal: Scarcity on Earth

5 When He opened the third seal, I heard the third living creature say, "Come and see." So I looked, and behold, a black horse, and he who sat on it had a pair of scales in his hand. 6 And I heard a voice in the midst of the four living creatures saying, "A quart of wheat for a denarius, and three quarts of barley for a denarius; and do not harm the oil and the wine."

Fourth Seal: Widespread Death on Earth

7 When He opened the fourth seal, I heard the voice of the fourth living creature saying, "Come and see." 8 So I looked, and behold, a pale horse. And the name of

> **him who sat on it was Death, and Hades followed with**
> **him. And power was given to them over a fourth of the**
> **earth, to kill with sword, with hunger, with death, and**
> **by the beasts of the earth. (Revelation 6:1-8)**

To many of us, the correlation between what Jesus had to say in Matthew 24 and these seals in the book of Revelation is readily apparent. The connection is very clear.

The first correlation is when Jesus says, *"Take heed that no one deceives you. 5 For many will come in My name, saying, 'I am the Christ,' and will deceive many" (Matthew 24:4–5)*. We'll see in a moment how that relates to the first seal, the rider on the white horse. Just remember the words "deceives" and "deception."

The second correlation is in the *"wars and rumors of wars" (Matthew 24:6)*, represented by the second seal and the red horse. Then, Jesus speaks of *"famines, pestilences, and earthquakes in various places" (Matthew 24:7)*, and famines are clearly represented by the third seal and the black horse, where measures of wheat and barley cost a full day's wages. Finally, earthquakes are mentioned a few times in the book of Revelation, the worst one is referenced in chapter 16, where John writes, *"And there was a great earthquake, such a mighty and great earthquake as had not occurred since men were on the earth (Revelation 16:18)*.

Just to provide further support to this correlation, Jesus continues in verse 9 of chapter 24: *"Then they will deliver you up to tribulation and kill you, and you will be hated by all nations for My name's sake. 10 And then many will be offended, will betray one another, and will hate one another" (Matthew 24:9–10)*.

This correlates with the fifth seal in chapter 6 of Revelation, which reads:

> **9 When He opened the fifth seal, I saw under the altar**
> **the souls of those who had been slain for the word of**

*God and for the testimony which they held. 10 And
they cried with a loud voice, saying, "How long, O Lord,
holy and true, until You judge and avenge our blood
on those who dwell on the earth?" (Revelation 6:9-10)*

The First Seal: Rider on the White Horse

So, now that we've correlated these seals with the words of Jesus in Matthew 24, let's look at the specific riders and horses in the first four seals, called the "Four Horsemen of the Apocalypse."

It begins with the rider on the white horse:

*And I looked, and behold, a white horse. He who sat
on it had a bow; and a crown was given to him, and he
went out conquering and to conquer. (Revelation 6:2)*

This first seal and the first rider on a white horse are the only seal, horse, and rider associated with a man. And this man is the antichrist.

Because he is on a white horse, many mistake him for Jesus Christ. After all, he has a crown on his head, and he is a conqueror. However, the key thing to remember about the antichrist and his actual coming is deception. He is riding a white horse, but unlike all of the westerns we see with the good guys riding white horses, this is not a good guy.

The key to understanding this time of the tribulation and the antichrist is deception, deception, deception, and more deception. I said it four times because Jesus also said it four times.

*4 And Jesus answered and said to them: "Take heed
that no one deceives you. 5 For many will come in My
name, saying, 'I am the Christ,' and will deceive many."
(Matthew 24:4-5)*

And then, a few verses later,

> *"Then many false prophets will rise up and deceive many." (Matthew 24:11)*

And then again in verses 23-24:

> *23 "Then if anyone says to you, 'Look, here is the Christ!' or 'There!' do not believe it. 24 For false christs and false prophets will rise and show great signs and wonders to deceive, if possible, even the elect." (Matthew 24:23-24)*

This is a masquerade. The antichrist is masquerading as the true Messiah. The rider on the white horse wears a crown, just as Jesus wears a crown. We mentioned before that he has in his hand a bow, but there are no arrows, signifying that he does not use weapons to acquire power but is more likely a brilliant politician, able to strategize and make dazzling political moves along with incredible charisma.

We'll talk about this character further in the next chapter, *"The Rise of The Antichrist."* However, this is not the only deception that is prophesied. Jesus starts off with the words, *"Take heed that no one deceives you" (verse 4),* and while false prophets and a false messiah are indeed deceptions, the devil has always used deception as a very powerful tool to fool individuals as well as nations.

I talked about deception in the last days in a previous chapter called *"Birth Pains."* As deception was the very first thing that Jesus wanted His disciples, His followers, to know, we could expect that deception is one of the things that we'll begin to see as we get closer and closer to the rapture, the tribulation, and the second coming (in that order). Jesus warns His disciples, and that includes all of us, that when we begin to see these signs, we should not be deceived.

The antichrist will come to power through deception. I believe that many of the problems that the antichrist will promise to solve will be propped up by deception. Politicians, government bureaucrats, and organizational leaders frequently use deception to sell and persuade a gullible and unprepared populace to buy-in to a problem, allowing the manufactured solution to be implemented without much resistance.

Fortunately for the elect who are present during the tribulation, Jesus gives assurances that they will not be deceived.

> *23 "Then if anyone says to you, 'Look, here is the Christ!' or 'There!' do not believe it. 24 For false christs and false prophets will rise and show great signs and wonders to deceive, if possible, even the elect. 25 See, I have told you beforehand." (Matthew 24:23-25)*

The Second Seal: Rider on the Red Horse

Let's continue with the second seal and the red horse.

> *3 When He opened the second seal, I heard the second living creature saying, "Come and see." 4 Another horse, fiery red, went out. And it was granted to the one who sat on it to take peace from the earth, and that people should kill one another; and there was given to him a great sword. (Revelation 6:3-4)*

While the first seal was the actual beginning of the tribulation, now that the second seal is opened, we have the "beginning of the end." Jesus describes these events, particularly in the first six seals, as "birth pangs." Just like a woman in labor, they start off relatively mildly but then get progressively worse and closer together.

Unlike the rider on the white horse, this second rider is not personified. There is no need to speculate about who he represents, as the message is in the color of the horse and what else is said. There are only two verses in this sixth chapter of Revelation that tell us about this rider on the red horse, but there are other verses in the Bible that we can use to fill in what the Scripture says about this event, this seal that is opened at the beginning of the tribulation, the beginning of the end. In this way, we will put into practice an important principle in Bible interpretation: we are all responsible for interpreting the Bible.

First, the one who is opening the seal is the Lamb, the Lord Jesus, Who was said to be worthy to open the seals in the previous chapter. These sequential seals, these birth pangs, are being opened by Jesus.

This rider on the red horse was granted the authority to take peace from the earth. Take note that the second seal removes peace from the earth. In actuality, war returns after a brief interval of peace.

The second seal follows the first. This rider on the red horse follows the first rider and the first seal, which are initially characterized by a short period of peace. This is part of the deception. If the antichrist promises world peace, it will not last long.

Peace returns momentarily to the Middle East, as the Bible mentions a peace treaty with Israel that will last only three and a half years, according to Daniel 9:27. And in any case, the world will fall for this promise of peace. The antichrist becomes famous for it; he is thought of as a natural leader, the one that can actually be trusted to rule and reign. Ultimately, he rules over ten kings (Revelation 17:12), but at the beginning of the tribulation, people will not recognize who he truly is. He will wait his time; he'll be patient, as he is a master deceiver. What we do know for sure is that when this second seal is opened, the peace and safety that the world is experiencing will be cut short. It could be that the peace that is "taken" actually propels the antichrist to a position of authority. People often turn to the government and leaders when their safety is threatened.

The Apostle Paul reminds his readers regarding this time of the end:

> *"For when they say, "Peace and safety!" then sudden destruction comes upon them, as labor pains upon a pregnant woman. And they shall not escape." (1 Thessalonians 5:3)*

Also, notice that when peace is taken away, this verse in Revelation 6:4 says, *"And that people should kill one another; and there was given to him a great sword."* We know that preceding and then during the tribulation, the Bible says there will be two specific military engagements. The War of Gog and Magog (Ezekiel 38) and the Battle(s) of Armageddon (Revelation 16:16) will take place specifically during the tribulation.

However, as the Scripture says here regarding this second seal, peace is taken. After seeing the violence during the pandemic and before the 2020 election in what are normally peaceful cities, we can see how the peace could be taken through violence, mob riots, brutality, and chaos. We have a clue that this will be true, as Jesus said that the end times would be like the days of Noah. Scripture says of the days of Noah, *"And Noah begot three sons: Shem, Ham, and Japheth. 11 The earth also was corrupt before God, and the earth was filled with violence. 12 So God looked upon the earth, and indeed it was corrupt; for all flesh had corrupted their way on the earth" (Genesis 6:10–12).*

We can now see how deception played a role in having the peace taken away in 2020. Most can recall that slogans, "identity politics," and "fake news" all had a role to play in the riots that were often called "peaceful demonstrations" by the mainstream media. The media and lawmakers often had a different point of view than what was clearly lawlessness.

We are living at a time when what the Scriptures say about the last days is becoming a reality. In the Apostle Paul's second letter to Timothy, chapter 3, Paul talks specifically of these days:

1 "But know this, that in the last days perilous times will come: 2 For men will be lovers of themselves, lovers of money, boasters, proud, blasphemers, disobedient to parents, unthankful, unholy, 3 unloving, unforgiving, slanderers, without self-control, brutal, despisers of good, 4 traitors, headstrong, haughty, lovers of

> *pleasure rather than lovers of God, 5 having a form of*
> *godliness but denying its power. And from such people*
> *turn away!" (2 Timothy 3:1-5)*

The color of this horse associated with the second seal is also important. The word "red" in this verse is the Greek word "*purrhos*," from the Greek word "*pur*," meaning fire. So, this word is often translated as "fiery red," and it's also the same color referenced for the dragon in Revelation chapter 12 that **"deceives the whole world" (Revelation. 12:9).**

In the Bible, the color red is full of symbolism and spiritual meaning. Red is often used in the Bible as a symbol of blood. As it's the color of blood, it's often a reference to atonement as well, since our atonement as believers in Jesus Christ is due to the blood of Jesus. For example, the red blood of the Passover lamb was applied to the doorposts as a sign that the angel of the Lord was to pass over the house.

The color red is also associated with our sins, as we can see clearly in the book of Isaiah:

> **Come now, and let us reason together,"**
> **Says the Lord,**
> **"Though your sins are like scarlet,**
> **They shall be as white as snow;**
> **Though they are red like crimson,**
> **They shall be as wool. (Isaiah 1:18)**

This is a good time to remind the reader and all of us that all of the people who go through the seven years of tribulation have not dealt properly with their sin problem. They have not been **"baptized into Christ"** nor have they **"put on Christ,"** as the Apostle Paul says in Galatians 3:27. If they had dealt with that sin issue, and come to Jesus, then all of them, both those alive and the dead, would have been caught up together in the clouds to meet the Lord in the air. (1 Thessalonians

4:17), prior to the beginning of the tribulation and the four horsemen and seal judgments. Those that dwell on the earth during the tribulation still have the opportunity to deal with their sin problem, and *"Though they are red like crimson, They shall be as wool" (verse 18).*

Note that this rider on the red horse was given a mighty sword. As I mentioned before, the rider is not personified; there is no specific person. The only identifiable person riding any of these horses is the rider on the white horse, which we have touched on briefly and will have more to say in the next chapter on the "Rise of the Antichrist."

The mighty sword mentioned here in connection with the second seal is interesting. In paintings and drawings dating back to the early Middle Ages, this sword is often represented by the artist as being very large and upright, like a warrior riding into battle.

What I find interesting is that the Greek words that are used and translated here as "mighty sword" can also be translated as "slaughter knife," a short sword or dagger mainly used for stabbing. This was the name for the short dagger that the Romans carried when they got up close and personal. According to my lexicon, it's (figuratively) an instrument for exacting retribution and depicts war and assassination, rebellion and revolt, and massacre.

This kind of dagger, combined with the fact that the Scripture says that people would slaughter one another (verse 4), reminds me of more than one incident in the Old Testament when the enemies of Israel suddenly began to kill each other. In 1 Samuel, we are told of a war with the Philistines, and the Scriptures say, *"Then Saul and all the people who were with him assembled, and they went to the battle; and indeed every man's sword was against his neighbor, and there was very great confusion" (1 Samuel 14:20).* The Scripture that speaks of this second seal and the rider on the red horse tells us that when peace is taken from the earth, people will slay one another. Whether that is by soldiers or mercenaries, armies or mobs, firebombs or bricks, guns or knives, peace will be taken from the earth, and all of this happens at the beginning of the tribulation. And what's even worse, while this happens at the beginning of the tribulation, this rider on the red horse doesn't go away! When we look at the remaining two horsemen of the Apocalypse, we will notice that their calamities are interconnected, and their reign of terror will most likely last through the seven trumpets and seven seals.

As we are talking about these seals, don't fall for the all-too-common explanation of this seal that the rider on the fiery red horse is already loose and that it is Russia, Communism, Islam, or Marxism. We heard the same thing when this COVID-19 pandemic began, and people were equating the COVID-19 pandemic with the famine that is represented by the fourth seal with the rider on the pale-green horse that brings death and pestilence, or epidemic and disease. This is nonsense and doesn't correlate with the proper conservative and historical exegesis of prophecy.

There are two main reasons why this type of interpretation of the book of Revelation is incorrect. First, Jesus describes the time of the Great Tribulation as a time unmatched from the beginning of the world until now and never to be seen again. Jesus says in Matthew 24:22, "***And unless those days were shortened, no flesh would be saved.***"

Communism, while an evil world system, doesn't represent the world-wide "taking of the peace" that is described. Also, COVID-19, while deadly, had literally no impact on the overall mortality rate. According to Dr. Zahia Ouadah-Bedidi, Research Professor at the Institute of Humanities and Social Sciences of the University of Paris, the COVID-19 mortality rate of 0.7%, with 80% of these deaths occurring in those over 70 years old, cannot be classified as a mortality crisis, nor does it have a significant impact on the global population.

(Source: International Day of Women in Science symposium, February 11, 2021 https://pressreleasenetwork.com "Will The Covid-19 Pandemic Impact Global Population Evolution?")

The second reason this type of interpretation of the book of Revelation is incorrect is because none of these seals will be opened, and none of the four riders of the apocalypse will be loosed until the beginning of the tribulation, which doesn't happen until after the church is *"caught up"* to meet the Lord in the air (1 Thessalonians 4:17) and the antichrist is revealed. The tribulation will last for a period of seven years, divided into two periods of 42 months, and that timing is specified a number of times in Scripture.

The Third Seal: Rider on the Black Horse

So far, we have seen the first seal and the rider on the white horse, whom we have identified as the antichrist. Then we discussed the second seal and the rider on the red horse, which spoke of the wars, the riots, and the violence. The Scripture regarding this rider on the fiery red horse said that it takes peace from the earth and makes people kill each other.

We'll continue now as we look at the third of the four horsemen, which refers to the first four riders on horses that we see in chapter 6 of the book of Revelation with the opening of seven seals. I mentioned when talking about the second horseman that the calamities spoken of in these first four seals are all interrelated, as the judgments and the reign of terror will likely continue through the entire seven years of the tribulation period. The third rider, horse, and seal begin in the book of Revelation in chapter 6, verse 5:

> *5 When He opened the third seal, I heard the third living creature say, "Come and see." So I looked, and behold, a black horse, and he who sat on it had a pair of scales in his hand. 6 And I heard a voice in the midst of the four living creatures saying, "A quart of wheat for a denarius, and three quarts of barley for a denarius; and do not harm the oil and the wine." (Revelation 6:5-6)*

In verses 5 and 6, we see the aftermath of wars and lawlessness; this is what happens when peace is taken from the earth. The Scripture says the rider on the black horse had a pair of balances, or scales, in his hand.

Today, we don't often see these types of scales or balances. However, for thousands of years, they were used in commerce as the way that things were weighed. The Scriptures use this language of scales and balances often. It speaks of justice, fairness, and impartiality. Proverbs 20:10 says, *"Diverse weights and diverse measures, They are both alike, an abomination to the Lord."*

If you recall the account recorded in the book of Daniel, King Belshazzar is having a feast and decides to use the articles from the temple in Jerusalem. A hand suddenly appears and begins to write the words: *Mene, Mene, Tekel, Peres.* The prophet Daniel interpreted these words as follows:

> *26 This is the interpretation of each word. MENE: God has numbered your kingdom, and finished it; 27 TEKEL: You have been weighed in the balances, and found wanting; 28 PERES: Your kingdom has been divided, and given to the Medes and Persians (Daniel 5:26-28)*

In more contemporary language and culture, "Lady Justice" is a common sight in courthouses and legal institutions. This woman, garbed in a tunic, has a pair of scales in her hand and typically wears a blindfold. She represents fairness and justice and is blinded because there is to be no partiality; the poor and lowly are to be provided the same justice as the rich and powerful.

Now we look again at the Scripture for today, and what do we see? The pair of scales, which we now understand as a symbol, and the Scripture continues: *"A quart of wheat for a denarius, and three quarts of barley for a denarius; and do not harm the oil and the wine"* *(verse 6).* On the wage scale at the time that John hears this voice, it was common for a person to receive one denarius for an entire day's work. And the Scripture says that this denarius would be the value of a measure of wheat and three measures of barley.

The literal explanation would mean that at this time, it would take an entire day's wages to buy a measure of wheat. A measure of wheat is one "dry quart," according to my conversion chart, and makes one and a half to two loaves of bread, enough for one good meal. Barley is neither as nutritious nor as desirable, and you could buy three meals of barley.

You can see why people often refer to this third seal, this rider on the black horse, as "**bringing fear**." Economics 101 tells us that with the supply and demand curve, when the supply is very scarce (as in a famine where people do not have adequate food supplies), the price is very high. So, we would say that this third seal, the rider on the black horse, is indicative of both very high prices (i.e., hyperinflation) and widespread shortages of food, as in a famine.

Back to Economics 101: At any given time, there is a balance between supply and demand. Food is produced, including not only wheat and barley but also milk, bread, eggs, cheese, flour, chicken, beef, and pork, as well as paper products, gasoline, building materials, medicines, and durable goods.

War and civil unrest disrupt that balance. Actually, we don't even need the real thing; all we need are rumors of war and impending disruption. Here in Florida, we know that during hurricane season, at any time, we can find the shelves of our stores empty; all the water, bread, batteries, and rope are gone. The shortage was caused by the rumor, or news report, of an impending hurricane.

We know here in Florida that many hurricanes that are thought to be a threat don't even come close. Who would have thought that the recent COVID-19 crisis would have immediately emptied the store shelves of toilet paper?

And this is the coming attraction of the movie that the book of Revelation is showing. The third seal and the rider with the red horse are pictures of hyperinflation, with rising prices for basic necessities. You see, it isn't that there is no wheat, no barley, no food, and no necessary supplies. If you want it badly enough, you'll have to pay for it. It will be so scarce that the price will be sky high.

We have seen that recently. When there was no toilet paper on the shelves of the local grocery store, you could go online at Amazon and buy it from third-party sources for 10, 20, or 100 times the normal price. Gasoline, when it is in short supply, doubles, and triples in price overnight. While this is something many have experienced, this third seal that lands the rider on the red horse likely brings hyperinflation, hunger, famine, and starvation on a global scale.

The Bible doesn't give us the specifics of why this happens. Many scholars look at the first two seals and the riders on the white horse and the black horse and see that wars and people killing each other are the likely causes, as we often see widespread famine after a war. While this is possible and likely, we have also seen what the weather, poor planning, and mismanagement can do.

For example, an early frost or a late freeze will cause fruit and vegetable prices to skyrocket. Centralized planning in Russia has caused numerous famines, and even today, as I write this chapter, there is talk of a famine because of disruptions in wheat production in the Ukraine. Back in the early 1930s, Russia was the world's second-largest producer of wheat (second only to the United States), but Joseph Stalin implemented a plan to replace Ukraine's small farms with state-run collectives. The plan failed miserably, leading to the 1932–1933 Ukrainian famine, known as the Holodomor. This word, "Holodomor," is supposedly a combination of the Ukrainian words for "starvation" and "to inflict death." Historians report that this famine, caused by the mismanagement of Joseph Stalin (whether intentional or accidental), claimed the lives of nearly four million people, or about 13% of the then present population in the Ukraine.

Let's stick with Russia for a minute, in particular communist Russia, the Soviet Socialist Republic, and we'll talk about the scarcity of consumer products combined with higher prices. Even when people had to queue for hours in Mosco to get bread, milk, and cheese, there was a black market that sold the same items at a much higher price. Interestingly, the prices were as high as an average worker's daily wage to buy food on the black market for himself and his family. At the same time, those in power, the rich, and the political leaders always had plenty.

Notice the Scripture also has these words: *"and do not harm the oil and the wine" (verse 6).* For some reason, Scripture (this voice that John hears) says that the oil and the wine will be left alone. I've read some commentaries, and one explanation is that there would be no money left to buy the oil and wine, which were considered essentials at the time of the Apostle John.

While that is a possible and good explanation, I call your attention to the truism that despite shortages, bans on certain products, and rationing, those in power, the rich, and the political leaders will always have plenty.

The Fourth Seal: Rider on the Pale Green Horse

In the book of Revelation, the Apostle John is shown the judgments of God that come upon the entire earth, and he sees a series of seven seals followed by a series of seven trumpets and then a series of seven vials or bowls. The first four of the seven seals are symbolized by four riders, each on a different colored horse. These four are also known as the Four Horsemen of the Apocalypse. The colors identified with these four horsemen in the first four seals are **White, Red, Black, and Pale Green.**

We've already taken a look at the first three seals that are opened, which signal the beginning of the tribulation. The first seal, the rider on the white horse, we identified as the Antichrist. The second seal, the rider on the red horse, takes peace from the earth and makes people kill each other. The third seal, the rider on the black horse that we said likely represented shortages of goods and services as well as hyperinflation and possibly famines, is the aftermath of wars and lawlessness; this is what happens when peace is taken from the earth. This third seal follows the second seal, which follows the first seal, and that first seal is the opening of the tribulation with the revelation of the antichrist.

So, let's continue and actually finish up this chapter on the Four Horsemen of the Apocalypse. This, by the way, is not the end of the seals, as there are a total of seven seals, and we'll address these remaining seals later. Let's go ahead and read the Scripture regarding the fourth seal, the rider on the pale horse:

> *7 When He opened the fourth seal, I heard the voice of the fourth living creature saying, "Come and see." 8 So I looked, and behold, a pale horse. And the name of him who sat on it was Death, and Hades followed with him. And power was given to them over a fourth of the earth, to kill with sword, with hunger, with death, and by the beasts of the earth. (Revelation 6:7-8)*

I mentioned earlier that some of the more contemporary events we have seen, from Hitler in the 1930s and 1940s to COVID 19 or the more recent double-digit inflation, are not **"tribulation worthy,"** meaning they lack the sheer destruction, horror, and catastrophic impact of what is foretold about the tribulation period. Here in the fourth seal, we see the ultimate impact of these judgments.

The fourth horseman of the Apocalypse has a name; none of the other horsemen do. His name is Death, and the Scriptures say that Hades accompanied him. Death comes riding on a pale horse, often translated as a "pale green" horse. The Greek word being translated here as pale or pale green is *chlrós*, which is the root of the word chlorine. In laboratories, hospitals, and forensics, chlorine dioxide, a yellowish-green gas, is the most commonly used disinfectant. Our morgues are kept clean and bacteria-free with the help of chlorine dioxide, which disinfects and eliminates odors. As a result, as we see in the Bible, chlorine dioxide is associated with death. Some of the ancient commentaries on these verses remarked that the yellowish-green color of the horse is the same as the yellowish-green color of a corpse.

This fourth horseman brings death and destruction to one-quarter of the world. No doubt much of the destruction originates like a domino effect from the first three seals: the antichrist on the white horse, the rider on the red horse who took peace from the earth, and the rider on the black horse who brings hyperinflation and famine.

The first four seals unleashed death and destruction, killing one-fourth of the world's population. If almost eight billion people are dwelling on the earth after the rapture, that means that nearly two billion people, or a quarter of mankind, could be killed by these four methods: *"with sword, with hunger, with death, and by the beasts of the earth" (verse 8)*

Some Bible scholars take the language to be symbolic primarily because of the overwhelming carnage that is represented by the death and destruction of one-fourth of the populace. However, God is deadly serious about bringing His judgment and His wrath to an unbelieving world. However, even with the devastation, there is hope. These same four methods of God's judgment were mentioned by the Old Testament prophet Ezekiel.

> *21 For thus says the Lord God: "How much more it shall be when I send My four severe judgments on Jerusalem—the sword and famine and wild beasts and pestilence—to cut off man and beast from it? 22 Yet behold, there shall be left in it a remnant who will be brought out, both sons and daughters; surely they will come out to you, and you will see their ways and their doings. (Ezekiel 14:21-22)*

God brought judgment on Jerusalem, but His promise was restoration. Despite the judgment and carnage during the tribulation, God's purpose is always to provide hope. Note the reference to wild beasts in both the Ezekiel prophecy as well as in Revelation 6:8. When the Babylonians took the people of Israel captive and Jerusalem was left desolate, wild beasts reclaimed the territory. We see this happen even today with villages and towns that are abandoned or deserted for any reason. Animals, including wolves, bears, big cats, and coyotes, reclaim desolate areas and establish their rule over the remaining human population.

These first four seals and the Four Horsemen represent God's judgment and wrath during the first half of the tribulation, a period of 42 months (Revelation 11:2 and 13:5–7), which is exactly 1,260 days (Revelation 11:3) and also represented as *"a time and times and half a time" (Daniel 7:25).* Jesus spoke specifically about this time.

> *7 For nation will rise against nation, and kingdom against kingdom. And there will be famines, pestilences, and earthquakes in various places. 8 All these are the beginning of sorrows. (Matthew 24:7-8)*

The beginning of sorrows is also referenced as the beginning of labor pains in 1 Thessalonians:

> *1 But concerning the times and the seasons, brethren, you have no need that I should write to you. 2 For you yourselves know perfectly that the day of the Lord so comes as a thief in the night. 3 For when they say, "Peace and safety!" then sudden destruction comes upon them, as labor pains upon a pregnant woman. And they shall not escape. (1 Thessalonians 5:1-3)*

These first four seals and the Four Horsemen represent the beginning of the Tribulation.

CHAPTER THIRTEEN
THE RISE OF THE ANTICHRIST

One of the major characters of the end times is the one known as the antichrist. Remember that Jesus Christ is the ultimate figure, as the end times culminate with the second coming of Jesus Christ and the book of Revelation's actual title is "The Revelation of Jesus Christ." However, the antichrist is an end time individual that is spoken of often in the Old Testament and the New Testament. The term "antichrist" is only found four times, and each time it is in the epistles of the Apostle John (1 John 2:18, 22; 4:3; 2 John 1:7). These verses in the epistles of John often refer to a specific person and many who have the same spirit. An example from 1 John:

> *"And every spirit that does not confess that Jesus Christ has come in the flesh is not of God. And this is the spirit of the Antichrist, which you have heard was coming, and is now already in the world." (1 John 4:3)*

This antichrist that is to come will deceive the world just prior to the time of Christ's second coming. Over the centuries, many have speculated on the identity of the antichrist, but the Bible is clear that he will not be revealed until the final seven years, called the tribulation, are about to begin. Much of the information we have on this individual comes from three sources: the Old Testament book of Daniel, Paul's letter to the Thessalonians, and the New Testament book of Revelation.

There are many who have a great fear of the antichrist. For some, that may be reasonable, as the antichrist will do the bidding of Satan for a period of seven years and become the ultimate world dictator. He will kill all those who oppose him or whom he believes are in the way of his ultimate objective. The antichrist's favorite method of capital punishment is beheading: ***"And I saw thrones, and they sat on them, and judgment was committed to them. Then I saw the souls of those who had been beheaded for their witness to Jesus and for the word of God, who had not worshiped the beast or his image, and had not received his mark on their foreheads or on their hand" (Revelation 20:4).*** His aim is to destroy Israel and those that are called saints, all individuals who refuse to take the symbol of the beast or the number of his name, "666."

However, for the present followers of Jesus Christ, there should be no fear at all when we speak of the rise of the antichrist. Jesus assured those who followed Him that they were not to be troubled. At the last supper, Jesus told His disciples,

> *1 "Let not your heart be troubled; you believe in God, believe also in Me. 2 In My Father's house are many mansions; if it were not so, I would have told you. I go to prepare a place for you. 3 And if I go and prepare a place for you, I will come again and receive you to Myself; that where I am, there you may be also."* **(John 14:1-3)**

This simple yet comforting statement by Jesus would have been understood differently by the disciples than we read it today. Jesus is clearly speaking of a future event, and he is using symbols and language from a Jewish or, more specifically, a Galilean wedding. Like a first century bridegroom who would leave his bride at her home in order to prepare a dwelling place for the new couple at his father's house, Jesus has gone to prepare a place for us.

When Jesus says, *"Let not your heart be troubled" (verse 1),* He is also echoing all of the promises made to His followers that not only will He return again, but just as importantly, He will return for His followers prior to the seven years of tribulation.

The tribulation begins with the opening of the seven seals. We have already spent some time looking at the first four seals and what is often called the "Four Horsemen of the Apocalypse," but as we are discussing the antichrist, we will have to revisit the first seal, where we first see the antichrist in the book of Revelation. The context of this first seal is the beginning of the tribulation, and we will see this first horseman in Revelation chapter 6.

> *1 "Now I saw when the Lamb opened one of the seals; and I heard one of the four living creatures saying with a voice like thunder, "Come and see." 2 And I looked, and behold, a white horse. He who sat on it had a bow; and a crown was given to him, and he went out conquering and to conquer." (Revelation 6:1-2)*

As we said earlier, this first seal and the first rider on a white horse are the only seal, horse, and rider associated with a man. And this man is the antichrist.

Because he is on a white horse, and because of all the television westerns we have seen with the good guys riding white horses, many mistake this initial rider for Jesus Christ. But Jesus said, *"Take heed that you not be deceived" (Luke 21:8),* and this individual on the white horse rises to become the end times world dictator through deception. The meaning of the term "antichrist" is simply "against Christ" or "another Christ."

The first mention of the antichrist in the book of Revelation says that he has in his hand a bow, but there are no arrows, signifying that he does not use weapons to acquire power. He is more likely a brilliant politician, capable of strategizing and making stunning political moves while displaying incredible charisma.

While medieval and even modern depictions of the antichrist portray something hideous and obviously evil, in all likelihood he will be especially well liked and will fool the people, the leader of the nations, and the Jews as well. If there were an election, the people of the world would vote for him. If there is an opportunity to give him power and rule, it will be given to him; it won't be seized.

By the time the Jews realize who he really is, it will be too late. We will most likely never know who the antichrist is if we are believers and alive before the rapture. Because I believe we are so close, I assume he is most assuredly already alive, already in some position of governance, and waiting for the opportunity for his plan to unfold.

Using the Bible as our primary reference, let's take a look at some clues we have regarding this individual, the antichrist. We'll also look at some scenarios that have been mentioned by other scholars and authors that would fit into what we know from Bible prophecy. Some of these scenarios are more speculative than others, but they do paint an interesting narrative.

The antichrist initially will not be a part of the ten world leaders that arise but will subdue or depose three of the ten and assume leadership: ***"I was considering the horns, and there was another horn, a little one, coming up among them, before whom three of the first horns were plucked out by the roots. And there, in this horn, were eyes like the eyes of a man, and a mouth speaking pompous words" (Daniel 7:8).***

Many were watching the European Commission as it began in 1951 with nine members and only needed one more for the ten that had been prophesied by Daniel. However, there are now 27 member nations, and while the ten world leaders obviously have a different literal fulfillment at some point in the future, many believe that Europe and possibly NATO will definitely have a large role to play in the kingdom of the antichrist.

- The antichrist is most likely alive today, possibly in politics, because of Jesus' words and warning of deception. Jesus told us that we needed to be wary of deception. *4 And Jesus answered and said to them, "Take heed that no one deceives you. 5 For many will come in My name, saying, 'I am the Christ,' and will deceive many" (Matthew 24:4-5).* Many political leaders have been pointed to as the antichrist recently, from Mikhail Gorbachev of Russia and his contemporary, President Ronald Reagan, to Volodymyr Zelenskyy of Ukraine and President Donald Trump. What do they all have in common, aside from the fact that none of them is the antichrist? They are all very charismatic and admired by the world!

- The antichrist will come to power by confirming a treaty that will bring peace to the Middle East and, in particular, Jerusalem. The treaty will allow the Jews to build a temple since we know the temple must exist for the antichrist to halt the sacrifices, i.e., *"he shall bring an end to sacrifice and offering" (Daniel 9:27).* Even today, the Temple Institute in Jerusalem is in the process of attempting to raise a red heifer that they believe will be necessary in purifying the new temple, specifically the ashes of the red heifer (Numbers 19:1–10).

- Many believe that the antichrist will come from eastern Europe, possibly Turkey, and could in fact be a Muslim. This is speculation, primarily because of the recent fury of radical Islam. However, the Bible does say that the antichrist will come from the people who destroyed Jerusalem in 70 AD: *"And the people of the prince who is to come shall destroy the city and the sanctuary" (Daniel 9:26).*

- The Bible says that the antichrist will change *"times and law" (Daniel 7:25),* and many quickly note that those who follow

Muhammad use a lunar calendar that began in 622 AD, when the Muslim prophet Mohammad migrated to Medina. So, for example, as I am writing this, the Muslim year is 1444 because the lunar year is eleven to twelve days shorter than the solar-based Gregorian year. In terms of "laws," Muslims today impose Sharia, or Islamic law derived from the teachings of the Quran and Muhammad.

- Many believe that the Old Testament prophet Zechariah indicates that the antichrist will have a damaged eye and a damaged arm: ***"Woe to the worthless shepherd, Who leaves the flock! A sword shall be against his arm And against his right eye; His arm shall completely wither, And his right eye shall be totally blinded" (Zechariah 11:17).*** However, this Scripture is not referring to the antichrist but to the false prophet, who is the false religious leader during the tribulation.

- The antichrist ***"shall regard neither the God of his fathers nor the desire of women, nor regard any god" (Daniel 11:37).*** There are numerous interpretations of Daniel's prophecy, and the context includes the fact that he has no regard for God or any god, for he shall exalt himself above them. Based on the worldwide rush in the 21st century to full acceptance of homosexuality, an openly gay antichrist would fit in well with the scenario of a man adored by the people who exalts himself and is in opposition to God's perfect plan for a man and a woman.

- In imitation of the resurrection of Jesus Christ, the antichrist will have been ***"wounded by the sword and lived" (Revelation 13:14).*** While Jesus literally rose from the dead, the antichrist's resurrection is a deception. The entire world is awestruck by the antichrist's alleged miraculous recovery. ***3 And I saw one of his heads as if it had been mortally wounded, and his*** *deadly wound was healed. And all the world marveled and followed the beast. 4 So they worshiped the dragon who gave authority to the beast; and they worshiped the beast, saying, "Who is like the beast? Who is able to make war with him?" (Revelation 13:3-4)*

- At some point, near the start of the second, three and a half year period known as the "Great Tribulation," the antichrist enters Jerusalem's temple. He is the one who, according to the Scriptures, *"opposes and exalts himself above all that is called God or that is worshiped, so that he sits as God in the temple of God, showing himself that he is God" (2 Thessalonians 2:4).* By this time, he has control of the world's economy, politics, and military power. All that is left is for those who dwell on the earth to bow down and worship him.

- The antichrist will hate the Jews and make war on them and the saints (often called the tribulation saints). The Bible is clear that God is the one who permits this, as the tribulation period is a time of wrath and judgment. The Bible says, *"It was granted to him to make war with the saints and to overcome them. And authority was given him over every tribe, tongue, and nation" (Revelation 13:7).*

- Those who do not worship the beast will be persecuted and killed; there will be many that are killed—the Bible calls it a great multitude, *"which no one could number, of all nations, tribes, peoples, and tongues" (Revelation 7:9),* that will over-come the antichrist, but by their own blood. *"And I saw thrones, and they sat on them, and judgment was committed to them. Then I saw the souls of those who had been beheaded for their witness to Jesus and for the word of God, who had not wor-shiped the beast or his image, and had not received his mark on their foreheads or on their hands. And they lived and reigned with Christ for a thousand years" (Revelation 20:4).*

- The antichrist will have supernatural powers as he will be indwelt by Satan. The Bible calls him *"the man of sin"* and *"the son of perdition" (2 Thessalonians 2:3).* Just as Jesus is the Son of God, the antichrist will be the son of Satan. Jesus' words in John chapter 10 describe perfectly how he is not the Christ but the antichrist! *"The thief does not come except to steal, and to kill, and to destroy. I have come that they may have life, and that they may have it more abundantly" (John 10:10).*

- The antichrist will become the ruler of the world and will have authority over every *"tribe, tongue, and nation" (Revelation 13:7).* The Bible never says "one-world" government, but the effect seems to be the same. Many conspiracy theorists talking about a "one-world" government may have been proven correct as the World Economic Forum speaks openly in their annual conferences of the need for a "New World Order." Klaus Schwab, founder and chairman of the World Economic Forum since 1971, openly promotes "The Great Reset" and "The Fourth Industrial Revolution," which would result in a world government that seems ripe for the antichrist's picking.

- A false prophet, called the second beast, joins the antichrist. *"Then I saw another beast coming up out of the earth, and he had two horns like a lamb and spoke like a dragon" (Revelation 13:11).* This false prophet leads a world religion that worships the image of the antichrist. This final world religion is called "Babylon," and the image of this false prophet is a *"woman seated on a scarlet beast" (Revelation 17:3).* This image of a woman on a beast is frequently used by the European Union, headquartered in Brussels. It can be found on the official Euro coin, as well as a postage stamp to commemorate the European Parliament, and as a statue right outside EU headquarters in Brussels. This is one reason we expect Europe and the EU to be active participants in both the antichrist and the false prophet.

- An image of the antichrist is set up, likely in the temple in Jerusalem, and the false prophet causes it to appear to be alive. *"He was granted power to give breath to the image of the beast, that the image of the beast should both speak and cause as many as would not worship the image of the beast to be killed" (Revelation 13:15).* What seemed like fantasy in the past is now commonplace at Disney's Magic Kingdom!

- This same false prophet causes everyone to take a mark like a tattoo: *"He causes all, both small and great, rich and poor, free and slave, to receive a mark on their right hand or on their foreheads, 17 and that no one may buy or sell except one who has the mark or the name of the beast, or the number of his name" (Revelation 13:16–17).* Many people saw the recent vaccine mandates as the "Mark of the Beast," but it couldn't be because there was no beast! The talk of making all currency digital at some point in the future would facilitate the necessity of an official mark in order to buy or sell.

- Together and empowered by Satan, the false prophet and the antichrist form an "unholy" trinity. This is all part of the counterfeit strategy of Satan in the end times. He desires to be worshiped, but his time is short. *"Woe to the inhabitants of the earth and the sea! For the devil has come down to you, having great wrath, because he knows that he has a short time" (Revelation 12:12).*

- The end of the antichrist after his brief reign of seven years is certain. The Bible clearly states that when Jesus returns to the earth with the armies of heaven, He consumes the antichrist with *"the breath of His mouth and destroy with the brightness of His coming" (2 Thessalonians 2:8).*

CHAPTER FOURTEEN
The Rapture of the Church

We are going to spend some time clarifying and defending the veracity of a very important Biblical truth, the "Rapture of the Church." We have mentioned the rapture a number of times and have already specified that it happens prior to the seven years of the tribulation. Later in this section, we'll be looking at two very key Scriptures, both of which are important parts of the Apostle Paul's teaching that were a mystery that was not known fully to the Old Testament prophets. The reason we say "not known fully" is because the rapture is in many ways another way of pointing to the future resurrection of believers. The resurrection of the body was an important and well-known teaching, a part of the old covenant, and mentioned by the Jewish followers of Jesus prior to His death on the cross and His own bodily resurrection.

For example, an important conversation between Jesus and Martha is recorded in the Gospel of John when Jesus delayed His arrival to help Lazarus and met Martha and Mary as He entered the village of Bethany.

21 Now Martha said to Jesus, "Lord, if You had been here, my brother would not have died. 22 But even now I know that whatever You ask of God, God will give You."

23 Jesus said to her, "Your brother will rise again."

> *24 Martha said to Him, "I know that he will rise again in the resurrection at the last day."*
>
> *25 Jesus said to her, "I am the resurrection and the life. He who believes in Me, though he may die, he shall live. 26 And whoever lives and believes in Me shall never die. Do you believe this?"*
>
> *27 She said to Him, "Yes, Lord, I believe that You are the Christ, the Son of God, who is to come into the world." (John 11:21-27)*

Martha and Mary were the sisters of Lazarus. We could continue in this reading of the Gospel of John and see how Jesus loved Lazarus and said in a loud voice, **"Lazarus, come forth!" (John 11:43)**; however, this is not the resurrection that Martha mentioned. Jesus did raise Lazarus from the dead, and while this was an amazing miracle to the joy of the family and all of Lazarus' friends in Bethany, it was not the resurrection that even Mary was referring to in her conversation with Jesus.

Martha summarizes very nicely what the Jews believed prior to Jesus' ministry regarding the truth of the resurrection. While Lazarus was dead, Martha believed that he would rise again on what she understood to be the last day. The word that is translated "last" in this verse is the Greek word *eschat*. It is where we get the theology word "eschatology," which is a compound Greek word with "*eschat*" (last) and "*logy*" (concerns), meaning the study in theology that is concerned with the end times and in particular the second coming of Jesus Christ.

Likely, the earliest reference to the resurrection in the last days was made by Job, a gentile (as he lived before Abraham), who the Bible tells us was from Uz, and that he was righteous and godly, blameless, and upright. Job was tested by God and harassed by Satan, but he continued to believe in God. In Job's fifth reply to his so-called friends, he says,

25 "For I know that my Redeemer lives,
And He shall stand at last on the earth;
26 And after my skin is destroyed, this I know,
That in my flesh I shall see God,
27 Whom I shall see for myself,
And my eyes shall behold, and not another.
How my heart yearns within me!" (Job 19:25-27)

Job believes that there will be a Redeemer. And Job states as a fact that even when he is dead and buried and no skin remains, his Redeemer will stand forth in the end times, and then, in his flesh (a resurrected body), Job will see God.

Nearly 1,500 years after Job, Isaiah prophesies of God's ultimate deliverance of His people.

But your dead will live, Lord;
their bodies will rise—
let those who dwell in the dust
wake up and shout for joy—
your dew is like the dew of the morning;
the earth will give birth to her dead. (Isaiah 26:19)

A third reference is from the Old Testament prophet Daniel, who wrote extensively in the latter days. Note that in these verses, Daniel includes both the righteous and the wicked in the resurrection.

1 "At that time Michael, the great prince who protects
your people, will arise. There will be a time of distress
such as has not happened from the beginning of nations
until then. But at that time your people—everyone
whose name is found written in the book—will be deliv-
ered. 2 Multitudes who sleep in the dust of the earth will

> *awake: some to everlasting life, others to shame and*
> *everlasting contempt." (Daniel 12:1-2)*

The quote from Daniel above is one of the reasons why scholars often reference Daniel in their study of the end times (eschatology). Daniel pulls this amazing teaching together, identifying the role of the Archangel Michael (the defender of Israel) in the end times, the fact that it is a time of great distress (the tribulation), and referencing a possible escape and the book of everlasting life.

The Apostle Paul's Teaching

When I began this chapter, I mentioned we would look at two very key Scriptures that were an important part of the Apostle Paul's teaching. One is in Paul's first letter to the Corinthians, and the context is that Paul is reminding this church of his earlier teaching on the resurrection. Paul was concerned because, while they believed that Christ rose from the dead and they believed in eternal life and a spiritual heaven, they were now beginning to deny the resurrection of the body based upon what they had been taught by their philosophers and not upon what the Bible and Paul clearly taught. Paul tells them,

> *12 "But if it is preached that Christ has been raised from*
> *the dead, how can some of you say that there is no resur-*
> *rection of the dead? 13 If there is no resurrection of the*
> *dead, then not even Christ has been raised. 14 And if*
> *Christ has not been raised, our preaching is useless and*
> *so is your faith." (1 Corinthians 15:12-14)*

Paul's argument is that if they know and believe that Christ was raised from the dead, how can they deny that all believers will be resurrected? Paul says their unbelief in a general resurrection negates their belief in the other, and as a result, their faith is useless.

I want to emphasize that Paul connects the bodily resurrection of Jesus Christ from the tomb on that Easter morning with a similar belief that we too will be raised from the dead. The Apostle Paul emphasized this connection between the two resurrections as a key teaching, stating that if there is no bodily resurrection, the divine plan of redemption crumbles.

Paul argues very convincingly that the resurrection is a historic fact. He contends that God's plan necessitates the resurrection of all believers, not just Christ. The whole redemptive plan is dependent on the bodily resurrection of Christ and of all who believe. Christ has risen, and so will we. It's the words of Jesus: "***Before long, the world will not see me anymore, but you will see me. Because I live, you also will live" (John 14:19).***

Before we go to what is really one of the two key verses on the rapture, let's pause for a moment and understand how Paul was arguing against culture, not against Biblical truth.

Grandma Dies and Joins Grandpa in Heaven

Today, if you listen to a conversation between people who supposedly believe that Jesus rose from the dead and believe in eternal life, there is rarely a mention of a resurrection. Likely, the conversation goes something like this: "*Yes, grandma has passed on and is now with grandpa in heaven. We know they are smiling down on us. Someday, we'll all be together and be able to see all of our friends and relatives in heaven.*"

This is our contemporary culture, and you'll see this sentiment often on television shows, in movies, and in books. The Apostle Paul would likely have a problem with it, just as he had a problem with the cultural beliefs that the Corinthians began to embrace. The problem is that believing in a heaven without embracing a bodily resurrection is not only contrary to our Christian faith but, as the Apostle Paul says, makes our faith useless.

History records that the early church rarely spoke about heaven but often spoke of the resurrection. In the Middle Ages in Europe, when people of wealth died, including nobles, kings, and queens, they were placed in a stone sarcophagus, and often the carving on the top would be of the deceased as they looked when they were in their early 30s. This well-known and accepted practice was based on the belief that in the resurrection, these individuals would be raised and would have a body that was in their 30s, similar to Jesus, as He was in His 30s when He rose from the dead.

Two major creeds of the church, the Apostles' Creed and the Nicene Creed, both dating back to the fourth century, speak definitely of the resurrection of the dead.

> *"I believe in the Holy Spirit, the holy Catholic Church,*
> *the communion of saints, the forgiveness of sins, the*
> *resurrection of the body, and life everlasting. Amen."*
> *(Apostles Creed)*

The Apostle Paul was concerned because, contrary to both Jewish and Christian teachings from the Bible regarding the bodily resurrection, there were Greek philosophers who taught that human beings were made up of body and soul. The body died and would decay, but the soul would live on forever. When Corinthian Christians said, "*There is no resurrection of the dead" (1 Corinthians 15:12)*, they were embracing these pagan ideas and assuming that even the body of Jesus had turned to dust but that His soul, as well as ours, remained immortal.

This is the first hurdle we have to address in order to fully understand the rapture. We need to, at the very least, come to the same understanding that Martha had to begin to embrace the Biblical teaching of the rapture.

The Apostle Paul continues in his letter to the Corinthians and tells them it is a mystery.

> *50 I declare to you, brothers and sisters, that flesh and*
> *blood cannot inherit the kingdom of God, nor does the*
> *perishable inherit the imperishable. 51 Listen, I tell*
> *you a mystery: We will not all sleep, but we will all be*

changed— 52 in a flash, in the twinkling of an eye, at the last trumpet. For the trumpet will sound, the dead will be raised imperishable, and we will be changed. (1 Corinthians 15:50-52)

Perhaps you have read or heard these verses in the past. The context is exactly the same as before. Paul was concerned because, while they believed that Christ rose from the dead, these Corinthians were embracing a Greek and pagan belief in the eternal state of the soul without a bodily resurrection. Paul reveals a mystery that wasn't known to even the Old Testament prophets. Paul is announcing how and when the resurrection of our bodies is to occur. This event is what is referred to as the rapture.

The rapture is the bodily resurrection of the believer. Collectively, all of the believers are known as "the church." The rapture, or resurrection, if you prefer, will happen *"in a flash, in the twinkling of an eye" (verse 52).* This letter was written to the Corinthians to encourage them and to give them comfort, just as it should encourage us and give us comfort as well. The Corinthians believed that Jesus rose from the dead, but they needed to believe that they too would rise. They had to believe that their flesh— their old bodies—would come back to life. People die, and Paul uses the word "sleep" just like Jesus did with Lazarus. In this context, sleep means being dead, but it also means being at peace. When you sleep, you dream, but your body rests. Paul says that *"we will not all sleep, but we will all be changed" (verse 51).* And everything will be altered at the same time by a single event. According to Paul, not everyone will sleep, indicating there will be a generation that is changed instantly from life to life!

All too often, our pastors find this too incredible to teach. It's much easier to teach that the faithful believer will go to heaven, and eventually all of those that we know who know Jesus too will be there as well. The rationale is that prophecy is messy, so just avoid it and be happy to have a nice church and the Ten Commandments, celebrate Christmas and Easter, and talk every now and then about heaven (and likely avoid hell).

But Paul was emphatic about this teaching. He says it is not enough to believe in heaven. We need to believe that our bodies will rise as well, just as Jesus rose from the dead, and we too will be changed.

So, this is called the resurrection of the believer, or the rapture. We'll see in a minute where this interesting word comes from. If people tell you they don't believe in the rapture, just let them know we all should believe in the resurrection of the believer. Don't get hung up on words that take on theological meanings beyond what they imply.

The rapture will involve an instantaneous transformation of our bodies to serve us for eternity, just as Jesus did!

> *"Beloved, now we are children of God; and it has not yet been revealed what we shall be, but we know that when He is revealed, we shall be like Him, for we shall see Him as He is."(1 John 3:2)*

So, let's specifically reference where this word "rapture" comes from in the Bible. The key verses we mentioned earlier are in 1 Thessalonians, chapter 4, verses 13–18. These are companion verses to 1 Corinthians chapter 15. In both epistles, or letters, Paul is teaching the people of God about death and the resurrection. We already talked about the confusion the Corinthians had, which was the reason for Paul's letter. For the Thessalonians, they were concerned that the believers who had died would somehow miss the resurrection, which Paul had taught them about earlier. Paul writes,

> *13 But I do not want you to be ignorant, brethren, concerning those who have fallen asleep, lest you sorrow as others who have no hope. 14 For if we believe that Jesus died and rose again, even so God will bring with Him those who sleep in Jesus.*

15 For this we say to you by the word of the Lord, that we who are alive and remain until the coming of the Lord will by no means precede those who are asleep. 16 For the Lord Himself will descend from heaven with a shout, with the voice of an archangel, and with the trumpet of God. And the dead in Christ will rise first. 17 Then we who are alive and remain shall be caught up together with them in the clouds to meet the Lord in the air. And thus we shall always be with the Lord. 18 Therefore comfort one another with these words. (1 Thessalonians 4:13-18)

So, where does the word "rapture" come from? It's in verse 17 above, in the English words "caught up" and the Latin translation of the Greek word "*harpazo*." St. Jerome began a translation of the Bible from Greek into Latin that would be known as the Latin Vulgate. It took St. Jerome 23 years, but his work was finished in 405 AD, and the Latin Vulgate stood as the only authorized Bible for over 1,000 years.

In the Latin Vulgate, the Greek word *harpazo*, which means "to snatch," "to be caught up with," or "to capture quickly," was translated by Jerome as "*rapiemur*," which is clearly related to our English words "rapture" or "raptured."

The Apostle Paul uses the word "sleep" six times in 1 Thessalonians, just as he did in his epistle to the Corinthians. Also, this event, called the rapture, impacts both those who have died as well as those that remain (those who are alive), and a trumpet sounds as the Lord appears and we rise in our new resurrected bodies.

The rapture is to be distinguished from the second coming. At the rapture, the Lord comes "*in the clouds*" to meet us "*in the air*" (1 Thessalonians 4:17). At the second coming, the Lord descends all the way to the earth to stand on the Mount of Olives, resulting in a great earthquake followed by the defeat of God's enemies (Zechariah 14:3–4).

The doctrine of the rapture was not taught in the Old Testament, which is why Paul calls it a "mystery" now revealed: ***"We shall not all sleep, but we shall all be changed— 52 in a moment, in the twinkling of an eye" (1 Corinthians 15:51–52).***

The rapture of the church is a glorious event that gives us hope. It's the event the virgins were waiting for in the parable Jesus told of the bridegroom who came at night in Matthew chapter 25. We will finally be free from sin. We will be in God's presence forever. There is far too much debate over the meaning and scope of the rapture. This is not God's intent. Rather, the rapture should be a comforting doctrine full of hope; God wants us to ***"comfort one another with these words" (1 Thessalonians 4:18).***

So the question is, when does this happen? Here's my overview based on what the Bible teaches:

1) **It's a global event.** It happens to many people—millions and millions of people all at the same time.

2) **It's not when you die.** Paul says, "We will not all sleep" (so it's an event independent of something after you die unless you are alive at that time).

3) **It's fast, in *"the twinkling of an eye"***—this is fast, but how fast we don't know, but many scholars believe it refers to the speed of light.

4) **It is imminent.** There are no events that need to happen first. Unlike the second coming, which comes after a number of events specified in the book of Revelation, the Bible teaches that the rapture can come at any moment. There is a doctrine called "imminence." It's a Greek word (aren't they all?) that means "something hanging over your head." Like a sign without any warning, Jesus could come back. We know this event well as ***"The Fullness of the Gentiles" (Romans 11:25).***

5) **It's a surprise.** Jesus remarked that *"of that day and hour no one knows" (Matthew 24:36).* Many have made a career of coming up with the date or day of the rapture, but Jesus said, "No one knows." For example, American Christian radio host Harold Camping predicted five different dates for the second coming, beginning on September 6, 1994, and ending on September 29, the same year, before predicting in 2005 that the date would be May 21, 2011. I remember well a popular book by Edgar Whisenant, a former NASA engineer, published in 1988, **"88 Reasons Why The Rapture Is In 1988."** It wasn't, and both Harold Camping and Edgar Whisenant have since died and are making no further predictions.

6) **It's a spectacular event.** I use the word "spectacular" because there are many who enjoy referring to this teaching as the "secret rapture," and they use these words as a pejorative. The rapture is certainly not a secret, as Paul has clearly articulated it, and it certainly isn't a secret to the vast majority of evangelicals and Biblical scholars. Detractors who call it "secret" will also be the first to say that the word "rapture" isn't in the Bible. We covered that untruth earlier and have identified why this spectacular event is when Jesus returns for His bride. It's spectacular in that it includes every believer, both those who have died and those who are still alive. After the rapture, there are a series of events over the next seven years that are also very clearly identified in scripture. These events all culminate with the second coming of Jesus Christ, which the Scriptures describe in terms that are significantly different from the rapture.

CHAPTER FIFTEEN

THE 70TH WEEK – THE TRIBULATION

This chapter has two theological terms that are related. The first is *"the 70th week,"* and the second is *"The Tribulation."* The correct Biblical viewpoint regarding the end times is that the 70th week (a term from the Old Testament prophet Daniel) is in fact the tribulation that is spoken of by the prophets and Jesus and described in detail by John the Apostle in the book of Revelation.

If this is correct (which we will demonstrate), then the tribulation period is a specific time period lasting one week of years, or exactly seven years. This distinguishes *"The Tribulation"* from any other distress, suffering, persecution, or period of agony experienced by believers in the past, present, or future. We will review this briefly, relying primarily on what the Scriptures tell us.

In the ninth chapter of Daniel, we read about the prophecy of the 70 weeks. It begins with Daniel having yet another vision of the Four Beasts, which provides more specificity into the four world kingdoms revealed in Nebuchadnezzar's dream in chapter 6. Daniel at this point is likely in his 80s, an older man, and he reads the writings and prophecies of Jeremiah and understands that the exile of the Jews to Israel was prophesied to last 70 years.

As Daniel begins to pray and fast, the Angel Gabriel comes to him and tells him something amazing. He tells him that while 70 years were the time of the exile, there would actually be 70 weeks (or *70 sevens*, the word for *weeks*) that are given to the people of Israel and the city of Jerusalem to bring about several things. Let's read what the Angel Gabriel had to say.

24 "Seventy weeks are determined
For your people and for your holy city,
To finish the transgression,
To make an end of sins,
To make reconciliation for iniquity,
To bring in everlasting righteousness,
To seal up vision and prophecy,
And to anoint the Most Holy.

25 "Know therefore and understand,
That from the going forth of the command
To restore and build Jerusalem
Until Messiah the Prince,
There shall be seven weeks and sixty-two weeks;
The street shall be built again, and the wall,
Even in troublesome times.

26 "And after the sixty-two weeks
Messiah shall be cut off, but not for Himself;
And the people of the prince who is to come
Shall destroy the city and the sanctuary.
The end of it shall be with a flood,
And till the end of the war desolations are determined.

27 Then he shall confirm a covenant with many
for one week;
But in the middle of the week
He shall bring an end to sacrifice and offering.
And on the wing of abominations shall be one who
makes desolate,

> *Even until the consummation, which is determined,*
> *Is poured out on the desolate." (Daniel 9:24-27)*

So, while this prophecy of the 70 weeks can be a little difficult at first, it starts to come together when you break it down with a little help from others who have studied it and written about it.

In verse 24, Gabriel says, "***Seventy weeks are determined for your people and for your holy city.***" Many translations use the words seventy "sevens," with the Greek word for seven representing the number of days in a week. In other words, a period of 490 years. We'll see in a minute that the object of this prophecy is the timing of the first coming of the Messiah, not the timing of the final seven years and His second coming.

Let's see how these seventy-sevens (weeks) of years, or 490 years, are broken up by the prophet Daniel:

> *"Know therefore and understand,*
> *That from the going forth of the command*
> *To restore and build Jerusalem*
> *Until Messiah the Prince,*
> *There shall be seven weeks and sixty-two weeks;*
> *The street shall be built again, and the wall,*
> *Even in troublesome times. (verse 25)*

These verses, while somewhat obscure, serve as a countdown clock for the arrival of Jesus, the Messiah. The Angel Gabriel said it "***shall be seven weeks and sixty-two weeks.***" As we already said that the week represents seven years, the prophecy could read, "***That from the going forth of the command to restore and build Jerusalem until Messiah the Prince (that is, the first coming of the Messiah, the Christ), there shall be 49 years, followed by 434 years, or a total of 483 years.***"

These prophecies of Daniel are spectacular! Scholars have determined that it was exactly 483 years from the time the command to rebuild Jerusalem was given by King Artaxerxes of Persia in c. 445

B.C. (see Nehemiah 2:1–8) to the time of Jesus' triumphal entry into Jerusalem (Matthew 21:1–9). The prophecy in Daniel 9 specifies that *"and after the sixty-two weeks, Messiah shall be cut off, but not for Himself" (verse 26).* This was fulfilled when Jesus was crucified.

The Angel Gabriel's prophecy also specified two time periods, the first being 49 years, which took us to the rebuilding of Jerusalem: *"The street shall be built again, and the wall, even in troublesome times" (Daniel 9:25).* This rebuilding is chronicled in the book of Nehemiah.

So... how does this fit in with the seven years of tribulation? I'm glad you asked!

Daniel was told there were seventy-sevens (weeks) of years, *"To finish the transgression, To make an end of sins, To make reconciliation for iniquity, To bring in everlasting righteousness, To seal up vision and prophecy, And to anoint the Most Holy (verse 24).* This verse references the time when God's kingdom will be fully established here on earth. Remember how Jesus taught his disciples to pray: *"Thy Kingdom come, thy will be done on earth as it is in heaven!" (Matthew 6:10)*

However, seventy-sevens are 490 years, and so far, the Jews have experienced a total of 483 years, but then Jesus was crucified. This was the end of this first series of sevens on God's stopwatch. 483 years, and *"Messiah shall be cut off" (verse 26).* Jesus died on the cross, rose from the dead, and ascended into heaven. The Holy Spirit then descended on Pentecost, and the church was born.

However, seven years remain. We can do the math: 490 years minus 483 years equals seven! The seven final years promised by the Angel Gabriel to the prophet Daniel for Israel

> *To finish the transgression,*
> *To make an end of sins,*
> *To make reconciliation for iniquity,*
> *To bring in everlasting righteousness,*
> *To seal up vision and prophecy,*
> *And to anoint the Most Holy. (verse 24)*

Notice that Daniel's prophecy contains a number of promises. I want to bring your attention to the two final promises, including *"to seal up vision and prophecy."* Sealing refers to both ending and fulfilling prophecy. This culminates with the glorious appearance and thousand-year reign of Jesus Christ, the Son of God.

"And to anoint the Most Holy" (verse 24)

Sometimes I refer to other translations, as occasionally a paraphrase sheds some additional light on a verse. This is particularly true with verse 24, as the simple, literal meaning of *"to anoint the most holy"* is a reference to a place, most likely the Millennial Temple. Here is the Message version of verse 24:

> *"Seventy sevens are set for your people and for your holy city to throttle rebellion, stop sin, wipe out crime, set things right forever, confirm what the prophet saw, and anoint The Holy of Holies." (verse 24, Message Bible)*

This is an amazing revelation given to the prophet Daniel by the Angel Gabriel. And it has been recorded all for us! There are some that will teach that all of these promises were fulfilled, ignoring the fact that there are still seven years remaining. However, a literal rendering of Daniel's prophecy indicates that there are seven years left.

God has reserved one last seven-year period for everything that must be accomplished. After the church, the bride of Christ, is taken to heaven, God turns his full attention back to the people of Israel. It is during these final seven years, the final week of the seventy weeks, that all the events occur during the time period known as the tribulation.

The Time Clock Begins!

The Angel Gabriel told Daniel that the clock would start at the time that a decree was issued to rebuild Jerusalem. Imagine a prophetic stopwatch that starts like the start of a race when the decree is made. We know from history that *"the going forth of the command to restore and build Jerusalem" (verse 25)* was given by King Artaxerxes of Persia c. 444 B.C. (see Nehemiah 2:1-8). The stopwatch starts after 49 years (7-sevens), after the walls and much of Jerusalem have been rebuilt, and it continues. Another 434 years pass (62-sevens), for a total of 483 years from the date King Artaxerxes says *"restore and build Jerusalem, "* to the time of Jesus, and the *"Messiah shall be cut off" (verse 26)*. The Messiah, Jesus of Nazareth, is crucified!

Click! The stopwatch is stopped; it's paused and waits for the next event.

The prophecy continues, and we see it fulfilled with the destruction of Jerusalem in AD 70. *"And the people of the prince who is to come shall destroy the city and the sanctuary. The end of it shall be with a flood, and till the end of the war, desolations are determined" (verse 26)*.

Verse 26 gives us a hint of the origin of the antichist. History has recorded that it was General Titus who conquered Jerusalem in AD 70. He was certainly a Roman. He went on to become the Roman emperor Titus Vespasianus Augustus (AD 79–AD 81). Most scholars agree that the *"prince who is to come"* is a reference to the antichrist, and *"the people of the prince"* is therefore a reference to Rome and the Roman Empire. Of course, since the Roman Empire stretched from Spain to Turkey and included much of the Middle East and northern Africa, it doesn't narrow down the prophecy to any particular group or nation.

The Tribulation

Daniel's prophecy, contained in the words of the Angel Gabriel in chapter 9, gives the exact moment when the stopwatch will begin again to count off the final seven years. Daniel adds the words, *"Then he shall confirm a covenant with many for one week" (verse 27).* Scholars believe that this likely refers to a peace treaty, possibly an agreement for a seven-year cessation of hostilities between the various nations and Israel. However, the antichrist violates the treaty halfway through the seven-year period: *"But in the middle of the week he shall bring an end to sacrifice and offering" (verse 27).*

The Great Tribulation, the final three and a half years, begins when the antichrist desecrates the temple halfway through the seven-year peace treaty, the *"covenant with many" (verse 27).*

The key to understanding this prophecy is that, of the 70 weeks of years, 69 have already been fulfilled. This leaves only one more "week" to be fulfilled. The past 2,000 years have been marked by a pause that gave rise to what we know as the Age of Grace or the Time of the Gentiles. The final seven years that are to be fulfilled are what is typically referred to as the tribulation. As I said above, the final three and a half years begin when the antichrist *"bring(s) an end to sacrifice and offering" (verse 27).*

In Matthew 24, Jesus gives us information that ties in directly with the prophet Daniel, with Jesus actually naming the prophet Daniel so that we would understand.

> *15 "Therefore when you see the 'abomination of desolation,' spoken of by Daniel the prophet, standing in the holy place" (whoever reads, let him understand), 16 "then let those who are in Judea flee to the mountains. 17 Let him who is on the housetop not go down to take anything out of his house. 18 And let him who is in the field not go back to get his clothes. 19 But woe to those who are pregnant and to those who are nursing babies in those days! 20*

And pray that your flight may not be in winter or on the Sabbath. 21 For then there will be great tribulation, such as has not been since the beginning of the world until this time, no, nor ever shall be. 22 And unless those days were shortened, no flesh would be saved; but for the elect's sake those days will be shortened." (Matthew 24:15-22)

Jesus specifically references Daniel and the *"abomination of desolation" (verse 15)*. At the time Jesus was speaking this prophecy, all of the scribes and the teachers of the law in Jerusalem believed that the prophecy had already been fulfilled in 156 BC, when a brutal Greek ruler, Antiochus Epiphanes, erected a statue of the Greek god Zeus in the temple in Jerusalem and then sacrificed a pig on the altar.

However, Jesus is drawing special attention to this prophecy and predicting that it will be fulfilled in the future. After the first three and a half years of the tribulation, the antichrist will reveal his true colors and desecrate the temple, abolishing sacrifice and offering (Daniel 9:27), and Jesus tells the remaining Jews to *"flee to the mountains" (Matthew 24:16)*, for the Great Tribulation has begun.

We'll conclude this brief look at the end of the tribulation period with the words of Jesus:

29 "Immediately after the tribulation of those days the sun will be darkened, and the moon will not give its light; the stars will fall from heaven, and the powers of the heavens will be shaken. 30 Then the sign of the Son of Man will appear in heaven, and then all the tribes of the earth will mourn, and they will see the Son of Man coming on the clouds of heaven with power and great glory. 31 And He will send His angels with a great sound of a trumpet, and they will gather together His elect from the four winds, from one end of heaven to the other." (Matthew 24:29-31)

CHAPTER SIXTEEN
THE TRUMPET JUDGMENTS

One of the interesting studies in theology is what is called Biblical Numerology. It is the study of the numbers that are in the Bible. Students of the Bible will find that certain numbers are often repeated and reveal patterns or types. However, most conservative scholars recommend caution when reading more into the numbers than what is clearly presented in the text.

Some of the numbers that are often repeated in the Bible are 40, 10, 7, and 3. For example, Jesus fasted in the wilderness for 40 days; the people of Israel wandered in the wilderness for 40 years; and Moses spent 40 days on the mountain. In all of these passages, the number 40 represents a time of preparation.

We could go through the other numbers and find similar commonality; however, we are now discussing the Trumpet Judgments, and in order to understand the Trumpet Judgments, we have to talk briefly about what the Bible says about the number 7. We first see the number 7 in Genesis and the days of creation.

1 Thus the heavens and the earth, and all the host of them, were finished. 2 And on the seventh day God ended His work which He had done, and He rested on the seventh day from all His work which He had done. (Genesis 2:1-2)

The number 7 is understood to have a number of meanings, primarily referring to completeness and perfection. In the book of Revelation alone, the number 7 is referenced over fifty times! It is the most significant number and provides a great deal of insight into this end time prophecy delivered by Jesus to the Apostle John that we call the book of Revelation. For example, chapter 1 of Revelation opens with a vision of seven stars and seven lampstands, and the angel tells the Apostle John they represent the seven churches. The sevens here represent the idea of completeness, just as the seven churches we mentioned earlier represent the entirety of the church age.

One of the most important references to the number 7 are the successive judgments introduced beginning in chapter 6 of Revelation, which include **the Seven Seals, the Seven Trumpets, and the Seven Vials.**

We have already talked at length about the seven seals that introduce the Four Horsemen of the Apocalypse (chapter twelve). In order to understand this series of judgments, we need to go back to the seventh seal as well as the words of Jesus in speaking of the tribulation.

The seventh seal is revealed at the beginning of the eighth chapter of Revelation. Chapter 6 of Revelation reveals the first six seals; chapter 7 is the vision of the four angels standing on the earth and the sealing of the 144,000 (we'll talk more about this in chapter eighteen of this book). Then, we turn to chapter 8 of Revelation, which deals primarily with the seven trumpet judgments, but it starts off with the seventh seal.

> *"When He opened the seventh seal, there was silence in heaven for about half an hour." (Revelation 8:1)*

How interesting that this seventh seal, after the seals that revealed war, famine, plague, pestilence, scarcity, widespread death, and martyrdom, results in *"silence in heaven for about half an hour" (verse 1).*

Remember that time periods in the Bible are often, but not always, symbolic and not literal. We do the same with time every day in contemporary English. For example, if we are called to dinner and we are almost ready, we may respond, "Give me a second," knowing and being understood that we will soon be joining everyone for dinner, but it will certainly be more than a second. This is what is being communicated when John writes, "***There was silence in heaven for about half an hour***" (***verse 1***).

The task is to understand the meaning of the words "***silence***" and "***half an hour.***"

The silence refers to the "***silence before a storm***," a colloquial saying that continues to be used today. The seal judgments are over, or at least have been described, and there is a pause before the trumpet judgments, which will be far greater and more devastating.

"***Half an hour***" is certainly a longer period of time than a second and, in all likelihood, refers to one-half of the entire tribulation period. The reference for this is actually in the book of Revelation, so it is a very good reference, as in Revelation 3, in the letter to the church of Philadelphia, it states,

> "***Because you have kept My command to persevere, I also will keep you from the hour of trial which shall come upon the whole world, to test those who dwell on the earth.***" (***Revelation 3:10***)

If the promise to the faithful in Philadelphia is to keep them from the hour of trial, and the hour of trial is understood to be the seven years of tribulation, then we would understand that half an hour is one-half of the tribulation, or roughly three and a half years.

We'll take a look at these trumpet judgments very soon, and we'll find that they are utterly devastating. They must occur near the end of the tribulation period, or no human life will be sustained. This is also what Jesus said about this final three and a half year period called the Great Tribulation.

21 For then there will be great tribulation, such as has not been since the beginning of the world until this time, no, nor ever shall be. 22 And unless those days were shortened, no flesh would be saved; but for the elect's sake those days will be shortened. (Matthew 24:21–22)

After the seventh seal is opened, John says there is a *"half an hour"* of silence: *"And I saw the seven angels who stand before God, and to them were given seven trumpets" (Revelation 8:2).* The seven trumpets of Revelation represent seven terrible judgments that will happen on the earth during the Great Tribulation. These judgments will overwhelm the biomes of this planet so completely that earth will not be able to recover without the intervention of God.

The opening of the seventh seal is actually the most important development and significant part of this prophecy thus far. The seventh seal is introduced by silence. Within the seventh seal are contained all of the subsequent developments culminating with the second coming of Christ. This will include the seven trumpets, followed a few chapters later by the seven bowls of the wrath of God.

The book of Revelation describes seven angels that sound seven consecutive trumpets, and each time a trumpet sounds, another judgment occurs.

These judgments are so devastating that scholars have a hard time assigning a chronological sequence or believing them to be literal. However, like the rest of the end time prophecies we've been discussing, these are real and will literally occur near the end of the tribulation. Jesus speaks directly to these judgments in chapter 21 in the Gospel of Luke.

25 "And there will be signs in the sun, in the moon, and in the stars; and on the earth distress of nations, with perplexity, the sea and the waves roaring; 26 men's hearts failing them from fear and the expectation of those things which are coming on the earth, for the

*powers of the heavens will be shaken. 27 Then they will
see the Son of Man coming in a cloud with power and
great glory. 28 Now when these things begin to happen,
look up and lift up your heads, because your redemption draws near." (Luke 21: 25-28)*

Jesus equates these judgments with His second coming. Note the
severity: *"men's hearts failing them from fear"* and the *"power of the
heavens will be shaken."* However, these judgments of God ultimately
culminate in the second coming of Jesus: *"Then they will see the Son of
Man coming in a cloud with power and great glory" (verse 27).*

The First Four Trumpets

As we saw earlier with the first four seals, often described as the
"Four Horsemen of the Apocalypse," the first four trumpets are often
uniquely grouped together. They are all contained in chapter 8, but the
reader should remember that these chapter and verse assignments orig-
inated in the 16th century and are not part of the original text.

Many scholars teach that the seals, trumpets, and bowls all describe
the same judgments but from different perspectives. However, in
looking at both the descriptions as well as the devastation of these different judgments, it is difficult to make a successful argument that these
seals, trumpets, and bowls all refer to the same or similar judgment. The
only possible explanation from this perspective (which I do not share)
is that these judgments are not to be taken literally but allegorically.

Let's take a look at the first four trumpets, and our text is the eighth
chapter of the book of Revelation, beginning with verse 6:

*6 So the seven angels who had the seven trumpets pre-
pared themselves to sound.*

7 The first angel sounded: And hail and fire followed, mingled with blood, and they were thrown to the earth. And a third of the trees were burned up, and all green grass was burned up.

8 Then the second angel sounded: And something like a great mountain burning with fire was thrown into the sea, and a third of the sea became blood. 9 And a third of the living creatures in the sea died, and a third of the ships were destroyed.

10 Then the third angel sounded: And a great star fell from heaven, burning like a torch, and it fell on a third of the rivers and on the springs of water. 11 The name of the star is Wormwood. A third of the waters became wormwood, and many men died from the water, because it was made bitter.

12 Then the fourth angel sounded: And a third of the sun was struck, a third of the moon, and a third of the stars, so that a third of them were darkened. A third of the day did not shine, and likewise the night. 13 And I looked, and I heard an angel flying through the midst of heaven, saying with a loud voice, "Woe, woe, woe to the inhabitants of the earth, because of the remaining blasts of the trumpet of the three angels who are about to sound!" (Revelation 8:6-13)

As if the first six seals were not enough—and remember, they included the appearance of the antichrist, followed by war, earthquakes, famine, and plagues—those who survive the six seals then must endure the trumpet judgments.

The text in Chapter 8 describes the first four trumpets, and as this is believed to be literal, it is clear that many will not survive. The remaining population of the earth (the Bible describes them as those who "***dwell on the earth***") may have survived, but life on earth has changed. The destruction from the first four trumpets is described as impacting "thirds," or actually "a third." One-third is referenced thirteen times in the chapter: 1/3 of the land, trees & grass *(verse 7)*.

- 1/3 of the sea creatures and ships *(verses 8 and 9)*

- 1/3 of the fresh water *(verse 11)*

- 1/3 of the sun, moon, and stars result in 1/3 of the light *(verse 12)*

The first four trumpets must occur in rapid succession, as the destruction and devastation are so catastrophic that few would survive long-term. The Bible describes those who remain behind to face these judgments as falling into two categories. The first are ***"those who dwell on the earth." (Revelation 11:10)*** This saying, referenced eight times in the book of Revelation, applies very broadly to all of those that remain on the earth after the rapture of the body of Christ (chapter fourteen in this book and referenced many times earlier). These people who dwell on the earth stand in opposition to God. Most stubbornly refuse to repent despite their knowledge that these judgments are from God. Even after the trumpets are sounded, they refuse.

> *20 But the rest of mankind, who were not killed by these plagues, did not repent of the works of their hands, that they should not worship demons, and idols of gold, silver, brass, stone, and wood, which can neither see nor hear nor walk. 21 And they did not repent of their murders or their sorceries or their sexual immorality or their thefts. (Revelation 9:20-21)*

The second category of people referenced in the book of Revelation is known by the word "*saint*." The Greek word is "*hagios*," literally meaning "*holy ones*," and they are mentioned fourteen times by the Apostle John.

These holy ones, or saints, are those who are not the object of God's wrath but must endure the wrath of the antichrist, the false prophet, and Satan himself. They will be oppressed, persecuted, and martyred. We see this when the Apostle John sees them as part of the fifth seal in chapter 6 of Revelation.

> *9 When He opened the fifth seal, I saw under the altar the souls of those who had been slain for the word of God and for the testimony which they held. 10 And they cried with a loud voice, saying, "How long, O Lord, holy and true, until You judge and avenge our blood on those who dwell on the earth?" 11 Then a white robe was given to each of them; and it was said to them that they should rest a little while longer, until both the number of their fellow servants and their brethren, who would be killed as they were, was completed. (Revelation 6:9–11)*

These "*hagios*," the "*holy ones*," during the tribulation who are martyred, are referred to by many scholars as the "**Tribulation Saints**."

This insight into the identity of these martyred believers is fundamental to rightly dividing the word of God and understanding what is going on during the tribulation period. The tribulation is a seven-year period of judgment directed at the wicked, with the opportunity for repentance and restoration available to anyone who believes the gospel. It is the time of God's judgment and wrath, and while the wrath is not directed towards the body of Christ (who will be raptured prior to the start of the tribulation), it will be a time when many that remain after the rapture will place their faith in Jesus Christ. The antichrist will persecute these new believers as well as the non-regenerate Jews during the tribulation, and many, if not most, will be martyred.

Therefore, these tribulation saints are those believers coming out of the Great Tribulation. They have overcome Satan and the antichrist by the blood of the Lamb and the word of their testimony (Revelation 12:11). The Apostle John sees these tribulation saints, a great multitude, standing before the throne of God and the Lamb, wearing white robes and holding palm branches (Revelation 7:9). The Apostle inquires of one of the elders as to who these men in white robes are. He is told, *"These are the ones who have survived the time of great distress; they have washed their robes and made them white in the blood of the Lamb" (Revelation 7:14).*

How did these tribulation saints hear the gospel in order to repent and believe? According to the seventh chapter of Revelation, in a vision given to the Apostle John between the sixth and seventh seals, there are a vast number of men—12,000 from the twelve tribes of Israel—totaling 144,000 who are sealed. In many ways, these 144,000 are one of the primary ways that the Lord brings the gospel to the house of Israel, as well as any others who would listen and believe. In addition, and most importantly, the Bible says there are two individuals of whom Jesus *"will give power to my two witnesses, and they will prophesy one thousand two hundred and sixty days, clothed in sackcloth" (Revelation 11:3).*

We have discussed the first four trumpet judgments and will need to continue with what the Bible reveals as the three woes to see the remaining trumpet judgments.

CHAPTER SEVENTEEN

THREE WOES!

And I looked, and I heard an angel flying through the midst of heaven, saying with a loud voice, "Woe, woe, woe to the inhabitants of the earth, because of the remaining blasts of the trumpet of the three angels who are about to sound!" (Revelation 8:13)

After the first four trumpet judgments, there is another pause in the narrative in Revelation. The trumpet judgments began in chapter 8 with *"silence in heaven for about half an hour (Revelation 8:1)*, and the first four trumpets followed. As we saw in the previous chapter of this book, these first four trumpets announce devastation described in thirds. We also saw that "a third" was referenced thirteen times in the first four trumpet judgments.

All of the seal judgments could be attributed to one man, the antichrist revealed in the first seal as the rider on the white horse. The trumpet judgments that follow, however, are unmistakably supernatural. Seven angels, who were given the seven trumpets, were all standing before God. What followed after the first four trumpets was an environmental catastrophe. Environmentalists and ecologists may opine about the survivability of the human race when a third of the land, a third of the trees, and a third of the grass are burned up and a third of our fresh water is gone. However, science cannot explain what truly happens during these trumpet judgments or their devastating impact, because what happens is supernatural.

Supernatural is the only way to describe what is announced by the eagle flying high overhead that cries out in a loud voice, **"Woe! Woe! Woe!" (verse 13)**. This announcement gives us an indication that the remaining trumpet judgments are significantly different, significantly more troubling, and significantly more dreadful than the first four. This is the meaning of the word "woe," which is used and repeated three times. The number three is most likely symbolically representing completeness, as in complete devastation, and is not necessarily assigning one woe to each of the remaining trumpets that are to sound.

The fifth and sixth trumpets immediately follow in the narrative that begins in chapter 9 of Revelation. The seventh trumpet, on the other hand, is completely different, beginning with a scene from heaven and a vision of God's temple, followed by the final judgments of the tribulation period known as the bowl judgments (to be described in chapter twenty of this book).

The fifth trumpet that sounds includes a rather lengthy narrative:

> *1 Then the fifth angel sounded: And I saw a star fallen from heaven to the earth. To him was given the key to the bottomless pit. 2 And he opened the bottomless pit, and smoke arose out of the pit like the smoke of a great furnace. So the sun and the air were darkened because of the smoke of the pit. 3 Then out of the smoke locusts came upon the earth. And to them was given power, as the scorpions of the earth have power. 4 They were commanded not to harm the grass of the earth, or any green thing, or any tree, but only those men who do not have the seal of God on their foreheads. 5 And they were not given authority to kill them, but to torment them for five months. Their torment was like the torment of a scorpion when it strikes a man. 6 In those*

*days men will seek death and will not find it; they will
desire to die, and death will flee from them.*

(Revelation 9:1-6)

The star that falls *(verse 1)* is in all likelihood an angel, perhaps even
a fallen angel, that opens the abyss. The abyss was referenced in the
Gospel of Luke in chapter 8 when the demons begged Jesus not to send
them into the abyss. It's a place where demon spirits are imprisoned, and
the key that is given unlocks this abyss, this deep pit, and the demons
come out. This is the same abyss where Satan will be imprisoned for a
thousand years during the reign of Christ on earth (Revelation 20:1-3).
Note that these demon spirits are pictured as locusts, possibly as a reference to what the prophet Joel had to say about the Day of the Lord.
In Joel 1 and 2, Joel describes the **chewing locust**, the **swarming locust**,
and the **consuming locust (Joel 1:4).**

While these could literally be locusts, they are definitely not natural locusts but supernatural beings, most likely demons. Interestingly,
while the first four trumpet judgments did their damage to the grass and
trees (Revelation 8:7), these creatures **"were commanded not to harm
the grass of the earth, or any green thing, or any tree, but only those
men who do not have the seal of God on their foreheads" (verse 4).**

I have mentioned a number of times that Scripture tells us that we,
the body of Christ, are not appointed to wrath, and here we see that
even during the darkest days of the tribulation, those with the **"seal
of God on their foreheads" (verse 4)** are exempt. This refers at least
to the 144,000 *(Revelation 7:4)* and possibly all believers that have not
taken the mark of the beast *(Revelation 13:16),* and of course those that
have already been martyred *(Revelation 6:10).* These demon locusts that
are released from the abyss have a king. Revelation 9:11 says that the
name of their king in Hebrew is **Abaddon** and in Greek, **Apollyon**. In
Hebrew, the name "Abaddon" means "place of destruction"; the Greek
title "Apollyon" literally means "The Destroyer."

While these names could refer to Satan, it is more likely that this king of the demon locusts is an underling, a specific demon who reports to Satan. The Bible gives us a few indications that both angels and demons are organized into different ranks. The Bible identifies the Angel Michael as an archangel (Jude 1:9), and there are likely other archangels. In Ephesians 6:12, the Apostle Paul writes about at least three different ranks of evil forces, including ***principalities, powers, and world rulers.***

Verses 7–10 could be a script that would be perfect for a screenplay or a blockbuster science fiction movie produced and directed by the likes of Michael Crichton (*Congo, Jurassic Park I, II, and III*) and James Cameron (*Terminator, Titanic, Avatar*).

> *7 The shape of the locusts was like horses prepared for battle. On their heads were crowns of something like gold, and their faces were like the faces of men. 8 They had hair like women's hair, and their teeth were like lions' teeth. 9 And they had breastplates like breastplates of iron, and the sound of their wings was like the sound of chariots with many horses running into battle. 10 They had tails like scorpions, and there were stings in their tails. Their power was to hurt men five months (Revelation 9:7-10)*

These images (***like horses, like gold, like the faces of men, like women's hair, like lions' teeth***), while awesome, are not to be taken literally, as the word "***like***" indicates that what is seen is in fact not what is depicted in reality. However, the total impact of this vision that John sees is cruel, awesome, and altogether spectacular. There is a dire warning back in verse 6 regarding this trumpet judgment: "***In those days men will seek death and will not find it; they will desire to die, and death will flee from them***" (Revelation 9:6).

The Second Woe

The second woe is revealed when the sixth angel blows his trumpet. A voice from heaven calls out, *"Release the four angels who are bound at the great river Euphrates" (Revelation 9:14).*

As the four angels were bound, we can safely assume that these are demons that rebelled with Satan at some point in the past. The key words that are operative here immediately follow:

So the four angels, who had been prepared for the hour and day and month and year, were released to kill a third of mankind. (Revelation 9:15)

The hour, day, month, and year have been known since time immemorial, a time established by God. We see why they had been imprisoned as well, because as soon as they are released, they kill a third of mankind.

This is about the fourteenth time in the trumpet judgments that *a third* is used to describe the extent of the devastation. However, this time the message is part of the second woe and is significantly different, significantly more troubling, and significantly more dreadful than any of the other thirds. Those that had been bound *"were released to kill a third of mankind. 16 Now the number of the army of the horsemen was two hundred million" (Revelation 9:15-16).* We can likely assume that the army of *two hundred million*, consisting of both horses and riders, is demonic, as the number is even greater than the number of men (and women) any country has ever mustered. During the First World War (WWI) and Second World War (WWII), the combined Allied and Central Powers (WWI) and Allied and Axis Powers (WWII) mustered a total of about 140 million soldiers. Notice that the Scripture repeats their impact and the killing of *"a third of mankind"* as the plagues of *"fire, smoke, and brimstone" (verse 17)* inflict the devastation. As there is no reason to understand a third of the human race as an allegory, this sixth trumpet results in the slaughter of nearly **two to three billion people** based on the present world population without trying to estimate the believers that would have been raptured prior to the tribulation.

Before we describe the third woe and the seventh trumpet, note that those who remain on the earth, the rest of the human race, do not repent.

> *20 But the rest of mankind, who were not killed by these plagues, did not repent of the works of their hands, that they should not worship demons, and idols of gold, silver, brass, stone, and wood, which can neither see nor hear nor walk. 21 And they did not repent of their murders or their sorceries or their sexual immorality or their thefts. (Revelation 9:20–21)*

The Third Woe and Seventh Trumpet

The third woe is revealed after an interlude in chapters 10 and 11 of the book of Revelation that introduces the two witnesses that we will discuss in the next chapter of this book.

> *14 The second woe is past. Behold, the third woe is coming quickly. 15 Then the seventh angel sounded: And there were loud voices in heaven, saying, "The kingdoms of this world have become the kingdoms of our Lord and of His Christ, and He shall reign forever and ever!" 16 And the twenty-four elders who sat before God on their thrones fell on their faces and worshiped God. (Revelation 11:14–16)*

The seventh trumpet and third woe are mentioned together; however, they apply to completely different prophetic events. When the seventh angel blew his trumpet, it signaled the time for the twenty-four elders (that we saw back in chapter 4 of Revelation) to announce the time of the end and the time of God's final judgment. This likely is not referring as much to the trials, plagues, and hardships during the tribulation as it is to the judgment after the tribulation on the nations and individuals, as well as the antichrist and false prophet. The time has been set; there will be no more delay.

The book of Revelation still has a number of chapters, and in those chapters, there are mysteries that will be revealed, followed by the seven bowl judgments that must happen at the very end of the Great Tribulation.

The seventh trumpet includes a brief look into the temple of God in heaven:

> *Then the temple of God was opened in heaven, and the ark of His covenant was seen in His temple. And there were lightnings, noises, thunderings, an earthquake, and great hail. (Revelation 11:19)*

This third calamity lasts until the Battle of Armageddon, as described in Revelation chapter 16. Scripture demonstrates that all seven bowl judgments culminate in a great earthquake, that is the earthly version of the heavenly earthquake emanating from the temple noted above.

CHAPTER EIGHTEEN
144,000 AND THE TWO WITNESSES

In this chapter, we group together both the 144,000 that are first mentioned in Revelation chapter 7 and the two witnesses that are mentioned in Revelation chapter 11. There are good reasons for this, as both of these groups are uniquely commissioned by God to proclaim the gospel and provide a witness for God. Both groups are also ultimately martyred for their faith, only to be brought to heaven to be rewarded.

While it is not known exactly when these two witnesses and the larger group of 144,000 will be commissioned and ordained, the majority of conservative Bible scholars believe that the 144,000 will be sealed early in the first half of the tribulation. Many others, as well as myself, also believe the two witnesses will minister during the same time, the first half of the tribulation. However, there are some great scholars like the late Dr. John Walvoord of Dallas Theological Seminary and others who believe the two are commissioned in the second half of the tribulation, called the "Great Tribulation."

As the first mention of these witnesses is in chapter 11, after the sixth trumpet, which most understand to be in the second half of the tribulation, the logic of Dr. Walvoord and others is sound. However, when I look at the narrative given, they seem to be killed by the antichrist as he begins to exercise supernatural power over the Jews still in Jerusalem. This places the timing of their execution by the antichrist at the midpoint of the seven years. Considering the two witnesses, Scripture says, *"And I will give power to my two witnesses, and they will prophesy one thousand two hundred and sixty days, clothed in sackcloth"(Revelation 11:3).* They would therefore appear at the beginning of the tribulation and likely be blamed for the plagues associated with the initial seals that are opened.

The 144,000

We can realize that the 144,000 are commissioned by God to serve as evangelists when we remember that one of the primary reasons for the tribulation is for the salvation of the Jewish nation. At the time of the rapture of the church, there will not even be one faithful witness left on earth, so it will be imperative that the 144,000 be commissioned early to be that witness, first to the Jewish nation but then also to those that remain on earth.

As faithful servants of our God, the 144,000 will do everything the Lord commands. As prophets of Jesus, they will have the seal of God on their foreheads and *"who follow the Lamb wherever He goes" (Revelation 14:4).*

These 144,000 are first introduced in chapter 7 of Revelation, which is actually a "flashback" prior to the opening of the seven seals in the previous chapter. The Scripture describes the four winds of heaven (Revelation 7:1), which is likely a reference to the four horsemen loosed in the first four seals. Two verses later, the angel's instruction seems to confirm this assumption that it happened prior to the first four seals.

> *1 After these things I saw four angels standing at the four corners of the earth, holding the four winds of the earth, that the wind should not blow on the earth, on the sea, or on any tree. 2 Then I saw another angel ascending from the east, having the seal of the living God. And he cried with a loud voice to the four angels to whom it was granted to harm the earth and the sea, 3 saying, "Do not harm the earth, the sea, or the trees*

> *till we have sealed the servants of our God on their fore-*
> *heads." 4 And I heard the number of those who were*
> *sealed. One hundred and forty-four thousand of all the*
> *tribes of the children of Israel were sealed:*
>
> *5 of the tribe of Judah twelve thousand were sealed;*
> *of the tribe of Reuben twelve thousand were sealed;*
> *of the tribe of Gad twelve thousand were sealed;*
> *6 of the tribe of Asher twelve thousand were sealed;*
> *of the tribe of Naphtali twelve thousand were sealed;*
> *of the tribe of Manasseh twelve thousand were sealed;*
> *7 of the tribe of Simeon twelve thousand were sealed;*
> *of the tribe of Levi twelve thousand were sealed;*
> *of the tribe of Issachar twelve thousand were sealed;*
> *8 of the tribe of Zebulun twelve thousand were sealed;*
> *of the tribe of Joseph twelve thousand were sealed;*
> *of the tribe of Benjamin twelve thousand were sealed.*
> *(Revelation 7:1-8)*

Understanding the background, the genealogy, or the nationality of these 144,000 is actually critical to the understanding of the entire book of Revelation and end times prophecy. If these tribes of Israel are not taken literally but symbolically, then the Jewish connection to end times prophecy is easily lost, and it quickly becomes allegorical. This leads to a misunderstanding and a denial of an actual seven years of tribulation, a denial of seven specific seals, seven specific trumpet judgments, and ultimately seven specific bowl judgments.

Revisiting my earlier key principle from chapter one of this book, as we read prophecy, we need to take the *"literal meaning when practical."* There is absolutely no reason to throw out something that is practical and can be taken literally. The twelve thousand sealed by the twelve tribes are repeated through each of the twelve tribes that are referenced.

The fact that one of the original tribes is missing (the tribe of Dan) is actually a further reason to take this literally.

While the Bible does not specifically tell us why the tribe of Dan is excluded from the list of the twelve tribes in Revelation 7, we can make an educated guess as we also see that the tribe of Manasseh is included, one of the two tribes that came from Joseph.

The twelve tribes of Israel typically refer to the twelve sons of Jacob: Reuben, Simeon, Levi, Judah, Dan, Naphtali, Gad, Asher, Issachar, Zebulun, Joseph, and Benjamin (Genesis 35). However, in the allotment of land, the tribe of Levi received no regular allotment as the priests served in the temple and administered six cities of refuge that provided asylum for those hunted for retribution. The two sons of Joseph, Ephraim and Manasseh, were adopted by Jacob as his own, providing Joseph literally a "double portion" in the allotment of land provided by Joshua nearly 400 years later.

If that isn't confusing enough, the Bible often refers to the entirety of the ten northern tribes as Ephraim. Ephraim had become the leading tribe of the northern kingdom, and Samaria was where the capital was located (Isaiah 7:9). Ephraim could have been included in the list of the twelve tribes but was not, while Joseph (his father) and Manasseh (his brother) were included.

Then, of course, is the curiosity regarding the omission of the tribe of Dan. While Scripture is silent as to the reason for the omission, we, like all theologians, can speculate.

Dan was allocated land by Joshua; however, Judges 18 describes a time when the tribe of Dan moved farther north into the area of Ephraim, and this includes the story of Micah and the idol that he made for the Danites to worship. While all of the northern tribes were involved with idolatry, the religious center of idolatry in Israel was located in the cities of Bethel and Dan. This is likely the reason that both Ephraim and Dan are missing from the list of tribes in Revelation 7. Of note, Dan is also missing from the genealogies in 1 Chronicles 1–9.

While no one today can claim to be of any particular tribe with any great certainty, the New Testament references the continued existence of the twelve tribes a few times. For example, the Apostle Paul, originally known as Saul, said that he was an Israelite, of the seed of Abraham, of the tribe of Benjamin (Romans 11:1). Most scholars understand that the Apostle Matthew was the same person as the tax collector, Levi, who, with that name, would have been of the tribe of Levi as well.

Jesus references the twelve tribes as well. For example, Jesus said to them, ***"So Jesus said to them, "Assuredly I say to you, that in the regeneration, when the Son of Man sits on the throne of His glory, you who have followed Me will also sit on twelve thrones, judging the twelve tribes of Israel" (Matthew 19:28).***

Both the kingdoms of Israel and Judah were conquered by the Assyrians in 722 BC and the Babylonians in 620 BC, respectively. However, by 515 BC, the people that returned from Babylon had rebuilt the temple (second temple) in Jerusalem. By this time, the majority of the people, but not all of the people, were from the tribe of Judah, and the name "Judah" as well as the name "Jew" stuck to represent any and all of the people of Israel.

It is interesting that today and since May 14, 1948, the Jewish nation is known as "Israel," not "Judah," perhaps as a partial fulfillment or precursor of this prophecy in Revelation 7.

What we know for certain is that at some point in the tribulation, likely early in the tribulation, God will select 144,000 servants, seal them, and protect them until their work is accomplished. These 144,00 servants will all be male, and the Scripture describes them as virgins. Most believe that their mission will be to proclaim Jesus Christ as Lord, the powerful truth of the gospel, and to bring as many as possible to salvation. Some authors writing on this subject have described them as "144,000 end time Billy Grahams," and I guess I just did as well. Many will come to know Jesus Christ as their Savior during the tribulation, thanks in large part to these faithful servants. These 144,000 are further described in chapter 14 of Revelation as the companions of the Lamb of God. As "*firstfruits*," they are described as martyred and victorious.

> *1 Then I looked, and behold, a Lamb standing on Mount Zion, and with Him one hundred and forty-four thousand, having His Father's name written on their foreheads. 2 And I heard a voice from heaven, like the voice of many waters, and like the voice of loud thunder. And I heard the sound of harpists playing their harps. 3 They sang as it were a new song before the throne, before the four living creatures, and the elders; and no one could learn that song except the hundred and forty-four thousand who were redeemed from the earth. 4 These are the ones who were not defiled with women, for they are virgins. These are the ones who follow the Lamb wherever He goes. These were redeemed from among men, being firstfruits to God and to the Lamb. 5 And in their mouth was found no deceit, for they are without fault before the throne of God.*

> *(Revelation 14:1-5)*

The Two Witnesses

Chapter 11 in Revelation introduces the two witnesses, and like one of our modern movies, this is a flashback to the beginning of the tribulation, and in this flashback, John is told to measure the temple. This temple that John measures is often called the "*Third Temple*" or the "*Tribulation Temple*." Many are looking for this temple to be built, as it will be an end times fulfillment and one of the signals of the beginning of the end.

It is called the third temple because Solomon built the first temple in the tenth century BC, and that temple was destroyed in the sixth century BC by the Babylonians. The second temple was built after Cyrus the Great, the King of Persia, and the Medes provided the decree for the Jews to return and to rebuild the temple. Zerubbabel began construction of the second temple around 525 BC, and that work is described in the Old Testament book of Ezra.

It was this temple, whose construction Zerubbabel oversaw, that was the center of worship for Israel except for a brief period of time in 156 BC, when a brutal Greek ruler, Antiochus Epiphanes, desecrated the temple by sacrificing a pig on the altar. This second temple was enlarged and fully renovated by Herod the Great and stood until 70 AD, when it was destroyed by the Romans.

As we read in the eleventh chapter of Revelation, the Apostle John is told to measure the third temple, and Jesus refers to His commission for the two witnesses to prophesy for 1,260 days, a total of 42 months, or three and a half years.

> *1 Then I was given a reed like a measuring rod. And the angel stood, saying, "Rise and measure the temple of God, the altar, and those who worship there. 2 But leave out the court which is outside the temple, and do not measure it, for it has been given to the Gentiles. And they will tread the holy city underfoot for forty-two months. 3 And I will give power to my two witnesses, and they will prophesy one thousand two hundred and sixty days, clothed in sackcloth." (Revelation 11:1-3)*

Presently, there are some very motivated people in Israel who are desiring to build this third temple. One of the obvious objections is that the site and the temple mount are presently occupied in large part by the Muslim *"Dome of the Rock."* It is possible that the reference in verse 2 above regarding the *"court which is outside the temple"* may indicate some arrangement whereby the Dome of the Rock and the third temple can coexist, at least for the duration of the *"twelve hundred and sixty days" (verse 3)*.

The third temple must exist at the midpoint of the tribulation, as the prophet Daniel refers to *"the prince who is to come" (Daniel 9:26)*. And this is the antichrist who will stop the sacrifices being offered in the temple at that time:

> *Then he shall confirm a covenant with many for one week; But in the middle of the week he shall bring an end to sacrifice and offering (Daniel 9:27).*

This prophecy by Daniel is also echoed by the Apostle Paul, who states that the antichrist will sit in this third temple and declare himself to be a god: *"who opposes and exalts himself above all that is called God or that is worshiped, so that he sits as God in the temple of God, showing himself that he is God (2 Thessalonians 2:4).*

So, the question is, "Who are these witnesses?" and "What do they do?"

Chapter 11 of Revelation tells us what they do:

> *5 And if anyone wants to harm them, fire proceeds from their mouth and devours their enemies. And if anyone wants to harm them, he must be killed in this manner. 6 These have power to shut heaven, so that no rain falls in the days of their prophecy; and they have power over waters to turn them to blood, and to strike the earth with all plagues, as often as they desire. (Revelation 11:5-6)*

The prophets have testified that there will be a time when God will deliver His people, Israel. These two prophets that appear at the beginning of the tribulation period will preach, and no one can stop them. Verse 5 says that *"fire proceeds from their mouth and devours their enemies.*" Presently, this time period prior to the tribulation, which is approaching 2,000 years, can be called the *"Age of the Church,"* but it is also the *"Time of the Gentiles."* Jesus says that *"Jerusalem will be trampled by Gentiles until the times of the Gentiles are fulfilled" (Luke 21:24).* In Romans 11:25, the Apostle Paul expresses the same understanding of the Gentiles' time, saying, *"Blindness in part has happened to Israel until the fullness of the Gentiles has come in" (Luke 11:25).*

So, God sends these two witnesses to preach primarily to the Jews. This is why they are stationed on the streets of Jerusalem. Like all of the prophets before them, they will be the target of persecution, but God supernaturally protects them for a period of 42 months, or 1260 days. If we take a look at the power that is given to them (*"fire proceeds from their mouth "* in *verse 5*; *"no rain falls"*; *"power over waters to turn them to blood, and to strike the earth with all plagues, "* in *verse 6*), we get a clue as to their nature, if not their identity.

These two witnesses are reminiscent of Moses, who was God's man during the ten plagues of Egypt (Exodus 7–12), and Elijah, who brought fire down from heaven (1 Kings 18 and 2 Kings 1). Interestingly, both Moses and Elijah are mentioned by name by the prophet Malachi, and the context is the Day of the Lord!

> *5 "Behold, I will send you Elijah the prophet*
> *Before the coming of the great and dreadful day*
> *of the Lord.*
> *6 And he will turn*
> *The hearts of the fathers to the children,*
> *And the hearts of the children to their fathers,*
> *Lest I come and strike the earth with a curse."*
> *(Malachi 4:5-6)*

It was also Moses and Elijah that appeared with Jesus, as recorded in the gospels of Matthew, Mark, and Luke, on the mountain top in the event called the Transfiguration. Here is what Matthew records regarding this event:

> *1 Now after six days Jesus took Peter, James, and John his brother, led them up on a high mountain by themselves; 2 and He was transfigured before them. His face shone like the sun, and His clothes became as white as the light. 3 And behold, Moses and Elijah appeared to them, talking with Him. (Matthew 17:1-3)*

Like the 144,000, these two witnesses are protected by the power of Almighty God until their mission is completed. It is completed at the midpoint of the tribulation, exactly 1260 days after the antichrist confirms a seven-year covenant with Israel (Daniel 9:27). When their mission is completed, the antichrist (called the beast) is able to overcome them.

> *7 When they finish their testimony, the beast that ascends out of the bottomless pit will make war against them, overcome them, and kill them. 8 And their dead bodies will lie in the street of the great city which spiritually is called Sodom and Egypt, where also our Lord was crucified. 9 Then those from the peoples, tribes, tongues, and nations will see their dead bodies three-and-a-half days, and not allow their dead bodies to be put into graves. 10 And those who dwell on the earth will rejoice over them, make merry, and send gifts to one another, because these two prophets tormented those who dwell on the earth.*
>
> *(Revelation 11:7-10)*

Note the utter joy of the non-redeemed and non-regenerate, the earth dwellers who have refused to *"repent of their murders or their sorceries or their sexual immorality or their thefts" (Revelation 9:21);* they throw a party! They send presents to each other, declare a feast, and likely all watch it on CNN or on their cell phones on social media! This unholy celebration could not have been fulfilled until these modern times, as the verse reads, *"those from the peoples, tribes, tongues, and nations will see their dead bodies three-and-a-half days, and not allow their dead bodies to be put into graves" (verse 9).* The two witnesses had been unstoppable for three and a half years, but now they have been lying in the street for three and a half days. But God is not done yet!

> *11 Now after the three-and-a-half days the breath of life from God entered them, and they stood on their feet, and great fear fell on those who saw them. 12 And they heard a loud voice from heaven saying to them, "Come up here." And they ascended to heaven in a cloud, and their enemies saw them. 13 In the same hour there was a great earthquake, and a tenth of the city fell. In the earthquake seven thousand people were killed, and the rest were afraid and gave glory to the God of heaven.*

> *(Revelation 11:11-13)*

While the unredeemed and unregenerated—those who have not repented—are watching the scene on the streets of Jerusalem on CNN or their cell phones, suddenly God sovereignly acts. The breath of life enters the dead bodies of the two witnesses, and they stand on their feet. Notice that what is heard by the two witnesses is the same as what the Apostle John hears at the very beginning of chapter 4 of Revelation. The Apostle John hears the words, *"Come up here!" (Revelation 4:1)* Hearing this, John is caught up into heaven and is immediately before the throne of God.

While some could speculate about what happened to the faithful after the rapture, as they are "here one moment and gone the next," the same cannot be said about these two witnesses. Scripture makes it clear that they went up to heaven in a cloud as their enemies looked on. This is similar to what the Apostles saw when Jesus ascended into heaven.

Although earthquakes, which are mentioned in verse 13, are more frequent in some areas of the world than others due to their potential for devastation, they are always a cause for concern. Several earthquakes are mentioned in the Bible, including one connected to Jesus' death and resurrection. These events mentioned in Scripture were not natural ones; rather, they were supernatural ones, just like the earthquake described in Revelation 11 will be. As a result, 7,000 people die, and one-tenth of Jerusalem is destroyed. While not as lethal as the one in China that occurred in the 16th century AD and left close to 850,000 people dead, this one achieved the desired outcome: ***"The rest were afraid and gave glory to the God of heaven" (verse 13).***

This is the first time in the book of Revelation that we see people giving glory to the God of heaven. Some identify those who gave glory to the God of heaven as being a part of the remnant, those Jewish believers who have come to salvation because of the preaching of the two witnesses. I hope this is true. On the other hand, the fact that they were terrified may indicate that we are not witnessing true repentance and regeneration, which cause them to give glory, but rather a response common to all who are suddenly confronted with the supernatural.

CHAPTER NINETEEN
THE MARK OF THE BEAST

T he thirteenth chapter of the book of Revelation describes the *Mark of the Beast*. The Bible describes it as a visible seal that the followers of the antichrist will willingly take in order to show their allegiance to him. It is the primary way that the antichrist controls the world's economy. However, it is the second beast that forces the people to take this mark. We cannot really discuss the *Mark of the Beast* until we first introduce the second beast.

> *11 Then I saw another beast coming up out of the earth, and he had two horns like a lamb and spoke like a dragon. 12 And he exercises all the authority of the first beast in his presence, and causes the earth and those who dwell in it to worship the first beast, whose deadly wound was healed. 13 He performs great signs, so that he even makes fire come down from heaven on the earth in the sight of men. 14 And he deceives those who dwell on the earth by those signs which he was granted to do in the sight of the beast, telling those who dwell on the earth to make an image to the beast who was wounded by the sword and lived. 15 He was granted power to give breath to the image of the beast, that the image of the beast should both speak and cause as many as would not worship the image of the beast to be killed.*

16 He causes all, both small and great, rich and poor, free and slave, to receive a mark on their right hand or on their foreheads, 17 and that no one may buy or sell except one who has the mark or the name of the beast, or the number of his name. (Revelation 13:11-17)

John sees the beast *"come up out of the earth" (verse 11)*. This beast has a different origin because instead of coming from the sea, he comes up out of the earth. While his origin is unknown, he is seen as having horns like a lamb and speaking like a dragon. The horns are an indication of who he pretends to be. Jesus is seen as a lamb nine different times in the book of Revelation, and here in this one verse, the beast out of the earth has two horns like a lamb. The *False Prophet* is the appropriate name given to him, as he appears like a lamb, gentle and lowly, but he speaks like a dragon. The words he uses are most likely a mix of truth and lies. However, even a half-truth is a total lie. It is Satan who empowers the false prophet, and together with the antichrist and Satan, these three become the unholy trinity of the tribulation.

Notice that the mission of the false prophet is revealed: *"He exercises all the authority of the first beast in his presence, and causes the earth and those who dwell in it to worship the first beast, whose deadly wound was healed" (verse 12)*. Satan, through supernatural powers or deception, provides the magic needed. First, the Scripture tells us that the antichrist's *"deadly wound was healed" (verse 12)*, mimicking the Lord's resurrection after His crucifixion. Further, the false prophet *"performs great signs, so that he even makes fire come down from heaven on the earth in the sight of men" (verse 13)*.

The people worship the beast because his mortal wound is healed and because of his supposed resurrection. Like God, he is seen to be omnipotent. The people cry out, *"Who is like the beast? Who is able to make war with him?" (Revelation 13:4)*

The chapter continues to say that the false prophet's deception includes making this idol, this image of the beast, breathe and speak.

Those who are not willing to worship this statue, this image of the beast, will be put to death. Like **Shadrach, Meshach, and Abednego,** who refused to worship the image of Nebuchadnezzar (Daniel 5), all who refuse to worship this image or take the mark of the beast on their right hand or forehead will be sentenced to death. Unlike Shadrach, Meshach, and Abednego, most, if not all, who refuse will be martyred.

Those who take the mark, either because they are deceived and truly worship the beast or because they fear death, all face a much worse fate:

> *9 Then a third angel followed them, saying with a loud voice, "If anyone worships the beast and his image, and receives his mark on his forehead or on his hand, 10 he himself shall also drink of the wine of the wrath of God, which is poured out full strength into the cup of His indignation. He shall be tormented with fire and brimstone in the presence of the holy angels and in the presence of the Lamb. 11 And the smoke of their torment ascends forever and ever; and they have no rest day or night, who worship the beast and his image, and whoever receives the mark of his name." (Revelation 14:9-11)*

What is the Mark?

No one knows exactly what this mark will look like. The Greek word for mark used in the text is *charagma*. It is used seven times in Revelation, always referring to this mark associated with the beast, also known as the antichrist. Strong's Concordance tells us the Greek word *charagma* is defined as a **stamp** or an **engraving**, more properly an engraving on a coin or a seal. This was thought to be a tattoo, as tattoos are etched or engraved marks on and beneath the skin. However, the recent technology of using microchips under the skin is now another way that this prophecy could be fulfilled. In keeping with one of the keys to understanding prophecy, we will assume there will definitely be a literal fulfillment, whether that is a ***microchip, a simple tattoo, or another visible mark***. Literal fulfillment means that the mark will be specifically on the right hand or the forehead. Some people speculate that an implanted microchip with all necessary personal information, including antichrist allegiance, would indicate that monetary currency would likely be digital, effectively controlling all buying and selling. While all of this is certainly possible, we do not want modern technology's advancement or adaptation to overshadow what the Scripture says.

Furthermore, many are concerned that they will take, or have already taken, some type of mark that literally marks their doom. However, the Scriptures tell us that this is a mark that people willingly take in the end times, and this mark of the beast is not fully implemented until the very end times, during the Great Tribulation, or the last three and a half of the seven years of tribulation. These people will take the mark because they identify themselves with the antichrist, they worship the antichrist, and they are on his team.

The ones that do not take the mark during the tribulation are primarily those whose names are written in the ***Book of Life.*** These are also known as the "***tribulation saints,***" whom Scripture says are sealed by God. The tribulation saints will not and cannot take the mark of the beast, and many will be killed; they will be martyred as a result.

The "***Mark of the Beast***" is one of the most discussed and least understood events or occurrences during the end times. Almost everyone has heard comments from those who should know better or who are completely uniformed, implying that some vaccine or modern technology is the mark of the beast. That should not come as a surprise because, back in the 1970s, we heard that the VISA™ credit card was the mark of the beast. This was later followed by the idea that the "www" of the world wide web was either the mark of the beast or at least the "***number of his name" (Revelation 13:18).*** More recently, it was the COVID vaccine that many suggested was the mark of the beast.

None of these, however, are the mark of the beast; they cannot be! There is no mark of the beast yet, because there is no beast. If there is no

The Apocalypse and Coming Kingdom

beast, there can be no mark of the beast. We know there is no beast yet, no antichrist yet—the one called the lawless one—because he is currently being restrained. The Scriptures tell us that clearly in 2 Thessalonians:

> *7 For the mystery of lawlessness is already at work; only He who now restrains will do so until He is taken out of the way. 8 And then the lawless one will be revealed, whom the Lord will consume with the breath of His mouth and destroy with the brightness of His coming. (2 Thessalonians 2:7-8)*

The Scriptures tell us that this man of lawlessness is being restrained, but at some point in the future, that restrainer will be taken out of the way. Some people think that "he" may be the Holy Spirit. However, we know that the Holy Spirit is omnipresent and that He cannot be taken out of the way, for He is everywhere. However, we (the body of believers) are temples of the Holy Spirit, and He lives within us. So, the Scriptures are giving us just one more hint (of many) that the body of Christ will be taken out of the way at what is referred to as the end of the "Age of the Gentiles," the "Return of the Bridegroom," and the "Rapture of the Church."

Before we leave this discussion of the mark of the beast, let me talk a little bit about some of these theories, often known as conspiracy theories, about the World Health Organization, the CDC, Bill Gates, Microsoft, the World Economic Forum, etc., that are already at work, pulling the strings that usher in the antichrist. There are many who say that the tribulation has already started, that the Four Horsemen of the Apocalypse are already at work, that the sign of the woman in the heavens has already been seen, etc.

Here's the thing: the tribulation period that the book of Revelation and the 70th week in Daniel chapter 9 describe as a seven-year period *does not begin* until the antichrist, the lawless one, the man of perdition, is revealed. This hasn't happened yet and won't happen until the restrainer is removed and the Lord comes for His bride. The Bible tells us, *"For God did not appoint us to wrath, but to obtain salvation through our Lord Jesus Christ" (1 Thessalonians 5:9).*

Secondly, we can see some similarities between end time prophecy and the recent technologies utilized, including the draconian and totalitarian responses to the coronavirus pandemic, including the global shut down of our businesses, our churches, and our schools, and the full-court press to require everyone to get "fully vaccinated" with an experimental COVID inoculation. All of this is likely a forerunner to the mark of the beast, but not the real thing.

Despots and tyrants have always tried to control the people they have the privilege to govern, and it's not a difficult stretch to see that this will include a mark that will be necessary to buy or sell. In the 1930s and 1940s, in Nazi Germany, everyone was required to carry their identification papers. Modern technology just shows us example after example of how this day that is spoken of by the Apostle John is quickly approaching.

"His number is 666"

Chapter 13 ends with these words and a reference to 666:

> *Here is wisdom. Let him who has understanding calculate the number of the beast, for it is the number of a man: His number is 666. (Revelation 13:18)*

Many ancient languages, such as Latin, Aramaic, Greek, and Hebrew, used letters as numbers or assigned numerical values to letters. Because that is not a practice in the English language, it's not as easy to relate to the concept of how to *"calculate the number of the beast" (verse 18).*

The word *gematria* refers to the practice of giving a number to a name, and the word *gematria* is Hebrew in origin. The text of the book of Revelation was written in Greek, and each letter of a name can be added up, resulting in a final sum, in this case in the name of the beast, the sum "666."

To complicate matters a little more, while there are only twenty-six Greek letters, after the tenth letter (*Iota*), which represents the number 10, the next letter (*Kappa*) represents 20 rather than 11. After the nineteenth letter, the letters then represent 200, 300, and so on. In this way, the letter "*Chi*" served as their number 600, "*Xi*" was their number 60, and "*stigmata*" was their number 6. Putting just these three letters together, you would come up with the sum of 666.

Was 666 a Coded Message?

There have been many Biblical scholars through the ages who have spent an excessive amount of energy and time trying to decipher this coded message of 666. After all, the Apostle John writes, "**Here is wisdom. Let him who has understanding calculate the number of the beast**" **(verse 18).** Once the beast is revealed, he will have a name that, in either Greek, Hebrew, or some other language, will add up to 666. As we can take a name, change it to the equivalent in Hebrew, Latin, or Greek, and add up the letters, it's always going to reveal a number, often 666. Using this method, many contenders for antichrist have been suggested, such as Henry Kissinger, a number of popes, religious societies, Napoleon, Hitler, or Caesar! Using some imagination, a number of names will work. For example, since the Apostle John was writing in the first century and Nero was on the throne, "Caesar Nero" will fit, and the number of that man is 666. However, you have to take a variant spelling of the Greek form of a Latin name, transliterated into Hebrew, to get to the desired outcome.

There are a couple of things we need to keep in mind in order to not cross over to the irrational or even wacko side when it comes to the number 666. The first is that the number 666 may indicate an **unholy trinity**. As 7 is the number of perfection and can also represent God, the number 6 is the number of man. 666 may be a human and demonic imitation of God, inherently falling short of the perfect and true. Seven is the number of completion and totality, and six doesn't quite make it.

The other thing to keep in mind that is actually much more important is that if you are a believer in Jesus Christ and are reading this, you will not be here when the antichrist is revealed. I mentioned earlier that the body of Christ is the one that is restraining the antichrist, and the Scriptures tell us that we will be removed, and taken up to be with Jesus prior to the tribulation (2 Thessalonians 2:6–8).

If you are not a believer and are still reading this, my question to you is, "What is holding you back?" The prophecies alone of the first coming of Jesus Christ should be more than sufficient to understand that the promise of a Messiah was fulfilled in Jesus Christ. He is the one who went to the cross to pay the penalty for your sins, which you could never pay. For *"whoever calls on the name of the Lord shall be saved" (Romans 10:13).* Don't hesitate, for the time is short.

The Apostle Paul speaks often of the coming of the Lord, and he calls it *"the blessed hope and glorious appearing of our great God and Savior Jesus Christ, 14 who gave Himself for us, that He might redeem us from every lawless deed and purify for Himself His own special people, zealous for good works" (Titus 2:13-14).*

In contrast to "the blessed hope," the prophets speak of "the Day of the Lord." This includes the entire tribulation period and the second coming of Jesus Christ; the Scriptures refer to it as a time of "great woe" and something to be feared!

The reign of the antichrist, the one associated with the mark of the beast and the number 666, is actually very short. From the time he is revealed to the time he is destroyed, it is no more than seven years. The Apostle Paul assures us: *"And then the lawless one will be revealed, whom the Lord will consume with the breath of His mouth and destroy with the brightness of His coming" (II Thessalonians 2:8).*

CHAPTER TWENTY
THE BOWL JUDGMENTS

"Then I heard a loud voice from the temple saying to the seven angels, "Go and pour out the bowls of the wrath of God on the earth."(Revelation 16:1)

There is a chronological structure to the tribulation events: *seven seals, seven trumpets, and the seven bowls* that together make up seven years of tribulation.

While many scholars do not take the seals, trumpets, and bowl judgments as separate judgments, there is enough difference in how they are described to convince many (including myself) that they are in fact distinct and, in all likelihood, sequential.

The seventh trumpet includes a scene change, and we see a vision of the Lamb standing with the 144,000 on Mount Zion. As Jesus doesn't return to Mount Zion until His second coming, this is a vision of the coming Day of the Lord, providing hope in the midst of the darkest time during the tribulation called the "Great Tribulation." Revelation 13:5 specifies a period of 42 months, or exactly three and a half years, for the Great Tribulation, thereby limiting the terrible reign of the Beast from the Sea, also known as the antichrist.

So, let's continue and take a look at each of the seven bowls that bring the ultimate end to the tribulation period.

First Bowl: Ugly Sores

So the first went and poured out his bowl upon the earth, and a foul and loathsome sore came upon the men who had the mark of the beast and those who worshiped his image. (Revelation 16:2)

Notice the obvious! This is the wrath of God, and this first bowl is directed to inflict it on those who have taken the mark of the beast or worshiped his image. While much of the tribulation's affliction and trouble affect everyone, regardless of their beliefs or nationality, this first bowl is specifically directed at those who have taken the mark of the beast.

The third angel, back in Revelation chapter 14, had given a warning against anyone who worshiped the beast and received the mark. This first bowl judgment is a partial fulfillment, as the greater fulfillment is their ultimate destination to be tormented with fire for eternity.

This bowl judgment is similar to Egypt's sixth plague of festering boils on both people and beasts. In that sixth plague in Egypt, the magicians could not replicate the plague nor alleviate it, unlike the plagues of water that became blood, the frogs, lice, or flies. Neither the antichrist nor the false prophet is able to do anything about the festering and ugly sores in the first bowl judgment. So much for the chant of the people, *"Who is like the beast? Who is able to make war with him?" (Revelation 13:4)*

Second Bowl: The Seas Turn Bloody

Then the second angel poured out his bowl on the sea, and it became blood as of a dead man; and every living creature in the sea died. (Revelation 16:3)

The devastation of the sea turning to blood and having every creature in it die is beyond imaginable. The ***"end of life as we know it"*** has arrived. While some expositors and theologians try to limit this event to the Mediterranean Sea, there is no hint in the text that this bowl judgment is in any way limited. The devastation is worldwide, which means two things. The first is that this bowl judgment period is short, very short. While the seven seal and seven trumpet judgments may have occurred over a period of three and a half years, these bowl judgments are likely to occur in quick succession at the end of the tribulation period. The second thing about the worldwide devastation caused by the sea turning to blood is that there will be a re-creation of the earth after Jesus returns. Some of the rebuilding will be done with the help of humans, both living and those in resurrected bodies, and some of it will be a recreation through Jesus speaking the word as He did in the manner described in Genesis.

Third Bowl: Rivers Turn to Blood

4 Then the third angel poured out his bowl on the rivers and springs of water, and they became blood. 5 And I heard the angel of the waters saying:

"You are righteous, O Lord,
The One who is and who was and who is to be,
Because You have judged these things.
6 For they have shed the blood of saints and prophets,
And You have given them blood to drink.
For it is their just due."

7 And I heard another from the altar saying, "Even so, Lord God Almighty, true and righteous are Your judgments" (Revelation 16:4-7)

This judgment, as with the previous bowl judgment, again involves the water supply. This time, it's the fresh water that turns to blood. Notice part of the reason for this particular judgment is given: *"For they have shed the blood of saints and prophets, And You have given them blood to drink. for it is their just due" (verse 6)*. Throughout the history of the church as well as the Jewish nation, our enemies have been "blood thirsty." Back in the sixth chapter of Revelation, during the seal judgments, the Apostle John sees a vision of souls under the altar that had been martyred for their faith during the tribulation:

> *And they cried with a loud voice, saying, "How long, O Lord, holy and true, until You judge and avenge our blood on those who dwell on the earth?" (Revelation 6:10)*

Because of their blood and the blood of untold millions of souls taken because of their faithful witness to God, no pure water will remain (except, of course, for the Fiji, Poland Springs, and Dasani kept securely and safely in the popular plastic bottles that environmentalists believe will lead to the ultimate destruction of our environment).

Fourth Bowl: Scorching Heat

> *8 Then the fourth angel poured out his bowl on the sun, and power was given to him to scorch men with fire. 9 And men were scorched with great heat, and they blasphemed the name of God who has power over these plagues; and they did not repent and give Him glory. (Revelation 16:8-9)*

Unlike the fourth trumpet, where one-third of the sun, moon, and stars are affected and their light is diminished by one-third, the fourth bowl impacts the sun by magnifying the sun's rays, so that people are burned by the scorching heat. Sunscreen and air conditioning will have little, if any, impact. As with some of the other plagues going back to the trumpet judgments, those who dwell on the earth do not repent. Instead, they blaspheme the name of the Lord and do not give Him the glory that is rightfully His. The literal Greek reading of this verse indicates that the people impacted here are the same people impacted by the first bowl: those that have taken the mark of the beast and worshiped his image. Believers will not be impacted. Those environmentalists I mentioned tongue-in-cheek earlier regarding their concern for plastic bottles also believe the earth is getting hotter. They are right, and they will be in for a shock when they find out how hot it actually gets!

Fifth Bowl: Darkness

> *10 Then the fifth angel poured out his bowl on the throne of the beast, and his kingdom became full of darkness; and they gnawed their tongues because of the pain. 11 They blasphemed the God of heaven because of their pains and their sores, and did not repent of their deeds. (Revelation 16:10-11)*

If you read these verses too quickly, you will miss some important points. Notice that the object of the wrath of this fifth bowl is the throne of the beast. It is his kingdom, his home turf, that plunges into darkness. One of the questions I often get is regarding Babylon, which is mentioned prominently in the book of Revelation in chapters 14, 16, 17, and 18.

There is some debate among scholars over whether Babylon in Revelation refers to a rebuilt Babylon on the Euphrates River or if it's a different place like Rome, New York City, or Riyadh, the capital city of Saudi Arabia, that has perhaps the greatest number of millionaires per capita of any modern city. In any case, the Babylon referenced in the book of Revelation, is the capital city of the antichrist. This is the location of the throne of the antichrist that will be thrown into darkness with the fifth bowl. This is similar to the ninth plague of Egypt, when God told Moses to stretch out his hand, and Egypt was cast into darkness, but the sons of Israel, who lived in Goshen, had light. This darkness only impacts the throne and kingdom of the beast.

Babylon To Be Rebuilt

Regarding the debate over a literal or symbolic Babylon, I believe and teach that the Babylon referenced in Revelation will be rebuilt and occupied by the antichrist during the tribulation on the Euphrates River. It will likely occupy the same site as the ancient capital, where the *Tower of Babel* was built in the land of Shinar. The prophet Zechariah records his vision of a woman in a basket in Zechariah 5:5–10, which is similar to the vision that John has of the woman on the beast in Revelation 17:1–6. The Old Testament prophets said regarding Babylon that it would be destroyed and never inhabited (Isaiah 13:2), that the foundational stones would not be reused, and that Babylon would be desolate forever (Jeremiah 51:26).

This prophecy has not yet been fulfilled! Babylon, which has lain in ruins for centuries, has been continuously occupied by Bedouins, and the stones used in this ancient capital city of the Chaldeans have been reused, a practice that continues to this day. Back in the 1980s, Saddam Hussein, the tyrant of Iraq, was fascinated by both Babylon and King Nebuchadnezzar, the Babylonian king who is featured prominently in the book of Daniel and sacked Jerusalem in 587 BC.

Saddam Hussein called himself the "son of King Nebuchadnezzar" and rebuilt much of the old Babylon meticulously and directly on top of the old ruins.

Much of Babylon was rebuilt by Saddam Hussein on its old foundation and was actually open to tourists after the fall of Iraq and Hussein in 2003. Hussein inscribed his name on many of the bricks, and had it not been for the American invasion of Iraq, Hussein may have moved his palace to a rebuilt Babylon. This is exactly what the antichrist will do in fulfillment of Bible prophecy. This Babylon will then fall, as it is prophesied in Revelation chapter 18:

> *1 After these things I saw another angel coming down from heaven, having great authority, and the earth was illuminated with his glory. 2 And he cried mightily with a loud voice, saying, "Babylon the great is fallen, is fallen, and has become a dwelling place of demons, a prison for every foul spirit, and a cage for every unclean and hated bird! 3 For all the nations have drunk of the wine of the wrath of her fornication, the kings of the earth have committed fornication with her, and the merchants of the earth have become rich through the abundance of her luxury." (Revelation 18:1-3)*

Babylon will be destroyed in one hour!

At the end of the seven-year period of tribulation, Babylon, the headquarters of the antichrist and the commercial capital of his kingdom, will be judged and destroyed. The text tells us that the kings and merchants of the earth were fully involved, as this was the central market for precious and expensive goods as well.

> *9 The kings of the earth who committed fornication and lived luxuriously with her will weep and lament for her, when they see the smoke of her burning, 10 standing at a distance for fear of her torment, saying, 'Alas, alas, that great city Babylon, that mighty city! For in one hour your judgment has come.'*
>
> *11 "And the merchants of the earth will weep and mourn over her, for no one buys their merchandise anymore:*

12 merchandise of gold and silver, precious stones and pearls, fine linen and purple, silk and scarlet, every kind of citron wood, every kind of object of ivory, every kind of object of most precious wood, bronze, iron, and marble; 13 and cinnamon and incense, fragrant oil and frankincense, wine and oil, fine flour and wheat, cattle and sheep, horses and chariots, and bodies and souls of men." (Revelation 18:9-13)

God has been patient, but, in the end, He will no longer tolerate the abomination, the evil, or the sinfulness of mankind. Notice in verse 10 that the fall comes in one hour, with the kings of the earth "***standing at a distance for fear of her torment" (verse 10)***. This is an apt and fitting description of a nuclear detonation that destroys people, buildings, landscape, and all goods and leaves the area radioactive and unapproachable for months, if not years.

There is another hint of a nuclear war in Zechariah's prophecy in chapter 14, and we will cover this and the final two bowl judgments in the next two chapters on Armageddon and the Second Coming of Jesus Christ.

CHAPTER TWENTY-ONE

ARMAGEDDON

The word Armageddon, like the word Apocalypse, is often misused but typically refers to a catastrophic battle or the annihilation of all human life. The word comes from the book of Revelation, and even when Armageddon is used by secularists, by people who don't believe what's in the Bible, the sense is that the Armageddon they refer to is the "biggie," the "third world war," and the end of the world.

Biblically, the word armageddon only appears once, in the sixteenth chapter of Revelation, and is associated with the Sixth Bowl, a judgment of God that is poured out during the second half of the seven years of tribulation.

Sixth Bowl: The Euphrates Dried

12 Then the sixth angel poured out his bowl on the great river Euphrates, and its water was dried up, so that the way of the kings from the east might be prepared. 13 And I saw three unclean spirits like frogs coming out of the mouth of the dragon, out of the mouth of the beast, and out of the mouth of the false prophet. 14 For they are spirits of demons, performing signs, which go out to the kings of the earth and of the whole world, to gather them to the battle of that great day of God Almighty.

15 "Behold, I am coming as a thief. Blessed is he who watches, and keeps his garments, lest he walk naked and they see his shame."

16 And they gathered them together to the place called in Hebrew, Armageddon. (Revelation 16:12-16)

In verse 12, the bowl is emptied on the river Euphrates, and we are told the reason: *"Its water was dried up, so that the way of the kings from the east might be prepared" (verse 12)*. To help the cause, three unclean spirits (read "demons") come out, one each from the dragon, the beast, and the false prophet. Here we see the unholy trinity in action, and they provoke the kings to gather their armies together for battle.

There has been a lot of speculation regarding who these *"kings from the east"* may be. As previously stated, Israel is the geographical center of prophecy; therefore, references to the north, east, and south are all references from the center, which is Israel, and more specifically, Jerusalem.

There is a very interesting prophecy in Daniel chapter 11 that helps explain these verses in Revelation. Daniel's prophecy is quite amazing, as it speaks prophetically and very clearly of the future battles between the Greek armies and the four generals that succeeded Alexander the Great *(Ptolemy, Seleucus, Cassander, and Lysimachus)*. These prophecies were written by Daniel in the sixth century BC with incredible accuracy, as they foretell the four divisions of Alexander's kingdom after his early demise in 323 BC in Babylon. The prophecy was remarkably (but only partially) fulfilled during Antiochus IV Epiphanes' (175–164 BC) reign. He was the notoriously vile and wicked ruler who killed thousands of Jews, desecrated the temple in Jerusalem by sacrificing a pig, and claimed to be Zeus incarnate (including taking the name Epiphanes, meaning "god manifest").

Armageddon described by Daniel

However, the prophecy of Daniel switches from the time of Alexander and the four generals to a future time that most futurists (this is the way we read the book of Revelation, as pertaining to the future and not yet fulfilled) understand to speak of the antichrist and the final battles leading to Armageddon. This all happens beginning in verse 35.

> *And some of those of understanding shall fall, to refine them, purify them, and make them white, until the time of the end; because it is still for the appointed time. (Daniel 11:35)*

The words *"until the time of the end"* give us the clue that there is a change in the timeframe. Also, Jesus very clearly indicated that the *"abomination of desolation"* that was partially fulfilled by Antiochus IV Epiphanes was also something that was still to come during the Great Tribulation.

Jesus speaking:

> *15 "Therefore when you see the 'abomination of desolation,' spoken of by Daniel the prophet, standing in the holy place" (whoever reads, let him understand), 16 "then let those who are in Judea flee to the mountains." (Matthew 24:15–16)*

Matthew 24, which is partially quoted above, is the quintessential discourse by Jesus that describes the calamities and woes associated with the tribulation period culminating with the coming of the Son of Man, Jesus Christ, in His glory!

> *Then the sign of the Son of Man will appear in heaven, and then all the tribes of the earth will mourn, and*

they will see the Son of Man coming on the clouds of heaven with power and great glory. (Matthew 24:30)

We started off this chapter with the sixth angel emptying his bowl on the river Euphrates, which prepared the way for the kings of the East. As we are talking about Armageddon, we need to clear up some misconceptions; they are relatively minor but important if we are to understand the kings of the East. Daniel chapter 11 is again key to helping us understand this final war, this gathering, and this assembling: *"And they gathered them together to the place called in Hebrew, Armageddon" (verse 16)*. Daniel's prophecy in chapter 11 involves primarily the king of the South and the king of the North, who we know as the antichrist.

> 40 *"At the time of the end the king of the South shall attack him; and the king of the North shall come against him like a whirlwind, with chariots, horsemen, and with many ships; and he shall enter the countries, overwhelm them, and pass through. 41 He shall also enter the Glorious Land, and many countries shall be overthrown; but these shall escape from his hand: Edom, Moab, and the prominent people of Ammon. 42 He shall stretch out his hand against the countries, and the land of Egypt shall not escape. 43 He shall have power over the treasures of gold and silver, and over all the precious things of Egypt; also the Libyans and Ethiopians shall follow at his heels. (Daniel 11:40-43)*

Again, please notice that the prophet Daniel is making it clear that these verses referenced above refer to *"the time of the end" (verse 40)*. Beginning with verse 40, the prophecy is referring to two different individuals or kingdoms: the king of the south and the king of the North. During the time of the Greeks and Antiochus IV Epiphanes (second century BC), the king of the south was Egypt, and the king of the North was Syria.

Gog and Magog

Some scholars speculate that, given these modern times, the king of the North is not Syria but Turkey or Russia. Russia is often the favorite and is mentioned by many scholars for two reasons. The first is prophetic. The prophet Ezekiel speaks of a coming war between nations *"from the far north,"* including the leader (king) and people known respectively as *"Gog of the land of Magog" (Ezekiel 38:2).*

The prophecy in Ezekiel 38 and 39 is amazing and very detailed and speaks of a short and very decisive war in the end times between a coalition of armies that likely include *Russia, Turkey, Ethiopia, Iran, Libya, and possibly Kosovo, Albania, and Bosnia-Herzegovina.* The names of the modern, often Muslim-majority nations have changed since Ezekiel's time, but all are now enemies of Israel and directly north of it.

The book of Revelation also mentions Gog and Magog gathering for battle after the Millennium and Satan are released.

> *7 Now when the thousand years have expired, Satan will be released from his prison 8 and will go out to deceive the nations which are in the four corners of the earth, Gog and Magog, to gather them together to battle, whose number is as the sand of the sea. 9 They went up on the breadth of the earth and surrounded the camp of the saints and the beloved city. And fire came down from God out of heaven and devoured them. (Revelation 20:7-9)*

Gog is not the King of the North

While trying to interpret the prophecies that involve Gog and Magog and their allies can be interesting, this war spoken of by Ezekiel in chapter 38 is not Armageddon but is likely an earlier battle either preceding the tribulation or at the very beginning of the tribulation. Gog is therefore not the king of the North; however, it is possible that Gog and Magog and all of these armies that are destroyed as described by Ezekiel in chapter 38 could re-arm, even seven years later, and form a coalition that is used by the antichrist in the battles we know as Armageddon.

The other reason that Bible scholars often incorrectly name Russia as the *"king of the North"* is because of their superpower status and their long history of involvement in the Middle East, particularly as of late with the withdrawal of American influence in Iraq and Afghanistan.

However, the real king of the North is none other than the antichrist. Antiochus IV Epiphanes was clearly a type of the ultimate antichrist in the context of Daniel 11. The prophecies regarding his invasion of the holy land, his desecration of the temple, and his declaring himself to be god were true for Antiochus IV Epiphanes and will be true as well regarding the antichrist. Jesus' warning in Matthew 24 to *"flee to the mountains" (Matthew 24:16)* should be taken literally.

The campaign typically known as the Battle of Armageddon begins with a battle between the king of the North (the antichrist) and the king of the south. Back in the second century BC, the king of the south was the Greek King of Egypt, but today it is likely an Arab confederation to the south of Israel that may still include *Egypt but also Saudi Arabia, Bahrain, and the United Arab Emirates.* These countries were included in the Abraham Accords, which were negotiated by representatives of US President Donald Trump in 2021 to normalize relations with the State of Israel and some Arab states.

The beginning of Armageddon (a series of battles) is told by Daniel beginning in verse 40 with the words *"at the end time."*

> **40 "At the time of the end the king of the South shall attack him; and the king of the North shall come against him like a whirlwind, with chariots, horsemen, and with many ships; and he shall enter the countries, overwhelm them, and pass through. 41 He shall also enter the Glorious Land, and many countries shall be overthrown; but these shall escape from his hand: Edom, Moab, and the prominent people of Ammon. 42 He shall stretch out his hand against the countries, and the land of Egypt shall not escape. 43 He shall have power over the treasures of gold and silver, and over all the precious things of Egypt; also the Libyans and Ethiopians shall follow at his heels. 44 But news from the east and the north shall trouble him; therefore he shall go out with great fury to destroy and annihilate many. 45 And he shall plant the tents of his palace between the seas and the glorious holy mountain; yet he shall come to his end, and no one will help him. (Daniel 11:40-45)**

These verses above refer to the final "king of the North," who, like Antiochus IV Epiphanes, will be full of arrogance, pride, and blasphemy and likely use this opportunity to move against Israel. The antichrist will reveal his true colors, desecrate the temple, and declare himself to be a god halfway through the tribulation period, which is exactly three and a half years, 42 months, or 1260 days, as prophesied. With this and with the help of the Holy Spirit, the eyes of the people of Israel will be opened. Some will flee, some will stay and fight, but by the end of this initial battle of Armageddon, the antichrist will overwhelm the Israel Defense Forces (IDF), defeat the coalition to the south that was allied with Israel, and *"shall stretch out his hand against the countries, and the land of Egypt shall not escape" (verse 42).*

Note verse 44, where it says, ***"But news from the east and the north shall trouble him; therefore he shall go out with great fury to destroy and annihilate many."*** For the first time, we see the armies of the kings of the east, which are mentioned in the sixth bowl judgment in Revelation 16:12. Apparently, Daniel includes in his prophecy a breakdown, civil war, or revolt within the world-wide kingdom of the antichrist, as he is disturbed when he hears of reports from the east and the north. He hurls his armies against this aggressor from the north and east and defeats the armies.

Some Bible teachers talk of an army of 200 million from the east, quoting Revelation 9:13–16. However, as we discussed in our chapter seventeen titled *"Three Woes,"* the ninth chapter of Revelation speaks of the sixth angel or sixth trumpet. The 200 million that were released to kill 1/3 of mankind were identified as demon spirits, not an army from the east.

While the antichrist is successful against this aggressor from the north and east, this is not the end of the war or the battle of Armageddon. Scripture tells us that the antichrist then makes his temporary headquarters somewhere between Jerusalem and the Mediterranean Sea, a distance of only 30 to 35 miles. The end of the antichrist comes soon after this, as he will surely and swiftly be destroyed by the coming of the King of Kings and the armies of heaven.

Revelation 19 is where we find the final battle of Armageddon and the end of the antichrist. These are the events associated with the second coming of Jesus Christ and will be further described in the next chapter.

Simultaneously, or perhaps immediately preceding the second coming of Jesus Christ, is the final bowl judgment, the seventh bowl.

Seventh Bowl: The Final Judgment

> *17 Then the seventh angel poured out his bowl into the air, and a loud voice came out of the temple of heaven, from the throne, saying, "It is done!" 18 And there were*

noises and thunderings and lightnings; and there was a
great earthquake, such a mighty and great earthquake
as had not occurred since men were on the earth. 19
Now the great city was divided into three parts, and
the cities of the nations fell. And great Babylon was
remembered before God, to give her the cup of the wine
of the fierceness of His wrath. 20 Then every island fled
away, and the mountains were not found. 21 And great
hail from heaven fell upon men, each hailstone about
the weight of a talent. Men blasphemed God because
of the plague of the hail, since that plague was exceed-
ingly great. (Revelation 16:17-21)

The seventh bowl reveals the universal and cataclysmic judgment on the earth. Jesus said that His coming was ultimately to be compared to the days of Noah:

26 "And as it was in the days of Noah, so it will be also
in the days of the Son of Man: 27 They ate, they drank,
they married wives, they were given in marriage, until
the day that Noah entered the ark, and the flood came
and destroyed them all. 28 Likewise as it was also
in the days of Lot: They ate, they drank, they bought,
they sold, they planted, they built; 29 but on the day
that Lot went out of Sodom it rained fire and brim-
stone from heaven and destroyed them all. 30 Even so
will it be in the day when the Son of Man is revealed."
(Luke 17:26-30)

Just as the flood during the days of Noah was universal and literally destroyed everything not saved on the ark, the seventh seal represents the final judgment. It is like the days of Noah, where God said, *"I will destroy man whom I have created from the face of the earth, both man and beast, creeping thing and birds of the air, for I am sorry that I have made them" (Genesis 6:7).*

While the Apostle John continues to see what Jesus reveals to him in chapters 17–19 after the seventh seal is poured out, there is no more wrath and no more judgment. The battles we know as Armageddon all conclude with the second coming of Jesus Christ and the seventh bowl.

CHAPTER TWENTY-TWO
The Second Coming

The second coming of Christ is the greatest promise remaining in Scripture. It is the ultimate fulfillment of the prophecies given to the people of Israel and, by extension, to the body of Christ. Jesus was born as a babe in Bethlehem and was the suffering servant in His first coming. In His second coming, Jesus is the conquering King, arriving with the saints and the armies of heaven at His side.

The term *"second coming"* is sometimes used to describe an amazing, stupendous, or astonishing event. In fact, newspapers reserve the largest type size available for only the most momentous occasions (i.e., "War is Declared" or "Men Walk on the Moon"). The largest type size used is called "second-coming type."

While the end times can be described as a period of time, the second coming is an event–the most amazing, stupendous, and astonishing event of all time–and the Bible describes this event in the book of Revelation.

> *Behold, He is coming with clouds, and every eye will see Him, even they who pierced Him. And all the tribes of the earth will mourn because of Him. Even so, Amen. (Revelation 1:7)*

At His second coming, Jesus fulfills all the roles the prophets of Israel described and hoped for in the Messiah: King of Kings and Lord of Lords, Great Ruler, Lawgiver, Prince of Peace, Mighty God, the Great Apostle and High Priest, the Chief Shepherd, and many more. Scholars have identified over 125 titles given to Jesus in the Bible. Revelation 1:7, referenced above, as well as Zechariah 12:10, indicate clearly that ultimately Israel as well as the entire world will recognize that it is Jesus who was pierced for the sin of mankind, and they will mourn. The Apostle Paul indicates that everyone remaining in the house of Israel will be saved.

> *25 For I do not desire, brethren, that you should be ignorant of this mystery, lest you should be wise in your own opinion, that blindness in part has happened to Israel until the fullness of the Gentiles has come in. 26 And so all Israel will be saved, as it is written:*
>
> *"The Deliverer will come out of Zion,*
> *And He will turn away ungodliness from Jacob;*
> *27 For this is My covenant with them,*
> *When I take away their sins." (Romans 11:25-27)*

Jesus will return to the land of Israel. Zechariah 14:4 identifies the location of the second coming as the Mount of Olives. Remember that when Jesus ascended into heaven, the Apostles and disciples were gazing up into the heavens, and then two angels spoke to the Apostles, *"Men of Galilee, why do you stand gazing up into heaven? This same Jesus, who was taken up from you into heaven, will so come in like manner as you saw Him go into heaven"* (Acts 1:11).

If we carefully examine all of the verses in the Bible that are directly related to Jesus' second coming, a clear picture begins to emerge. His second coming is addressed in great detail in Revelation 19:11-16.

As I mentioned in the previous chapter, this all happens either simultaneously or immediately following the seventh bowl judgment. This is how the Apostle John describes the second coming:

11 Now I saw heaven opened, and behold, a white horse. And He who sat on him was called Faithful and True, and in righteousness He judges and makes war. 12 His eyes were like a flame of fire, and on His head were many crowns. He had a name written that no one knew except Himself. 13 He was clothed with a robe dipped in blood, and His name is called The Word of God. 14 And the armies in heaven, clothed in fine linen, white and clean, followed Him on white horses. 15 Now out of His mouth goes a sharp sword, that with it He should strike the nations. And He Himself will rule them with a rod of iron. He Himself treads the winepress of the fierceness and wrath of Almighty God. 16 And He has on His robe and on His thigh a name written:

KING OF KINGS AND
LORD OF LORDS.

17 Then I saw an angel standing in the sun; and he cried with a loud voice, saying to all the birds that fly in the midst of heaven, "Come and gather together for the supper of the great God, 18 that you may eat the flesh of kings, the flesh of captains, the flesh of mighty men, the flesh of horses and of those who sit on them, and the flesh of all people, free and slave, both small and great."

19 And I saw the beast, the kings of the earth, and their armies, gathered together to make war against Him who sat on the horse and against His army. 20 Then the beast was captured, and with him the false prophet who worked signs in his presence, by which he deceived those who received the mark of the beast and those who worshiped his image. These two were cast alive into the lake of fire burning with brimstone. 21 And the rest were killed with the sword which proceeded from the mouth of Him who sat on the horse. And all the birds were filled with their flesh. (Revelation 19:11-21)

These verses in the book of Revelation, portraying the second coming of Jesus Christ, answer the question asked earlier by those dwelling on earth about the beast: *"Who is like the beast? Who is able to make war with him?" (Revelation 13:4)* There is actually no comparison, as Christ returns and easily defeats the beast, the false prophets, and the enemies of God.

This amazing vision that the Apostle John witnesses is full of symbolism:

- *A white horse*, the symbol of purity and of victory

- *Eyes were like a flame of fire*, symbolizing righteous judgment

- *On His head were many crowns*, the emblem of the King of Kings

- *Name written that no one knew*, speaks of His position and authority

- *A robe dipped in blood*, we must never forget that it was through His blood that we are redeemed. Also, the prophet Isaiah spoke specifically of the blood of His enemies:

2 Why is Your apparel red,
And Your garments like one who treads in the winepress?
3 "I have trodden the winepress alone,
And from the peoples no one was with Me.
For I have trodden them in My anger,
And trampled them in My fury;

> *Their blood is sprinkled upon My garments,*
> *And I have stained all My robes.*
> *4 For the day of vengeance is in My heart,*
> *And the year of My redeemed has come. (Isaiah 63:2-4)*

While symbolism abounds in these verses and much of Revelation, the event, the return, and the conquest of both the beast and the false prophet, as well as all the enemies of God, are to be taken literally.

The Armies of Heaven

Many people who read the book of Revelation are surprised to learn that the second coming of Jesus is accompanied not only by warfare and annihilation but also by the mention of the armies of heaven. "*And the armies in heaven, clothed in fine linen, white and clean, followed Him on white horses*" *(Revelation 19:14).*

While the angelic hosts were present at Christ's first advent, when He was born as a baby and the angel announced His birth to the shepherd and "a multitude of the heavenly host" began to praise God, at His second advent, the armies of heaven that accompany Jesus have a different mission. The Greek word that is translated "*armies*" is "*strateuma*," which is translated in the Bible as "*armies*," "*an army*," "*soldiers*," and "*troops*." This is consistent with the reference earlier in verse 11, "*He judges and makes war.*" While angels have often been dispatched to earth to be used in spiritual warfare, they have also been mighty in battle, as in 2 Kings 19:35, when the "*angel of the Lord went out, and killed in the camp of the Assyrians one hundred and eighty-five thousand.*" With the second coming, the armies of heaven will not only include the angels but also all of God's people, the saints. We saw them earlier in the same chapter 19, at what is called the Marriage Supper of the Lamb.

The Marriage Supper of the Lamb

To fully comprehend Jesus Christ's return with the armies of heaven, we must accept the Biblical truth that the bride of Christ has been removed from the earth prior to the tribulation period. All of those who were martyred during the tribulation period are then joined together with the faithful that were raptured prior to the tribulation.

> *9 When He opened the fifth seal, I saw under the altar the souls of those who had been slain for the word of God and for the testimony which they held. 10 And they cried with a loud voice, saying, "How long, O Lord, holy and true, until You judge and avenge our blood on those who dwell on the earth?" 11 Then a white robe was given to each of them; and it was said to them that they should rest a little while longer, until both the number of their fellow servants and their brethren, who would be killed as they were, was completed. (Revelation 6:9-11)*

At some point during the tribulation, these martyred souls, as well as the pre-tribulation saints who were caught up into heaven to be with Jesus (as we discussed at length in this book in *Chapter 14: The Rapture of the Church*), come together at what is known as the "Marriage Supper of the Lamb."

This theological and end times understanding of the Marriage Supper of the Lamb is critical because it provides continued support for the distinction between Israel and the church, as well as support for the "Age of Grace" and the "Rapture of the Church."

Jesus refers to Himself as the bridegroom in the Gospel of Mark in response to a question about fasting. Jesus answered them, *"Can the friends of the bridegroom fast while the bridegroom is with them? As long as they have the bridegroom with them they cannot fast. 20 But the days will come when the bridegroom will be taken away from them, and then they will fast in those days" (Mark 2:19-20).*

The concept of the Marriage Supper of the Lamb is best understood considering the wedding customs in Israel at the time of Christ. As you may recall, Joseph and Mary were "betrothed," but they had not yet come together as a married couple. Today, people are first engaged and then married at some point later in a public ceremony. The wedding custom in ancient Israel was a three-step process.

First, an arrangement was made by the parents of the bride and bridegroom. Often, the two desiring to be married would enter into an agreement and sign it with their parents, and then the parents of the bride were paid a dowry, or bride price. This custom is found in many cultures and continues to this day. In some cultures, it is the groom's parents who receive the dowry. The ancient tradition in Israel was to pay the bride's parents, as we see in the story of Jacob and his father-in-law, Laban, for providing service for seven years.

> *Now Jacob loved Rachel; so he said, "I will serve you seven years for Rachel your younger daughter." (Genesis 29:18)*

The execution of this agreement and the payment of the dowry began what is called the "betrothal period." This is the stage that Joseph and Mary were at in the wedding process when Mary was told by the angel that she would conceive a son by the power of the Holy Spirit (Matthew 1:18).

The second stage of the wedding process usually occurs about a year after the betrothal. During that year, the bridegroom would have returned to his father's house and prepared an addition, a structure or dwelling place, for himself and his new bride.

Jesus references this second step when speaking to his disciples about his soon-coming departure and return.

> *1 "Let not your heart be troubled; you believe in God,*
> *believe also in Me. 2 In My Father's house are many*
> *mansions; if it were not so, I would have told you. I*
> *go to prepare a place for you. 3 And if I go and pre-*
> *pare a place for you, I will come again and receive*
> *you to Myself; that where I am, there you may be also."*
> *(John 14:1-3)*

At the end of this time, the father of the bridegroom would turn to his son and say, "Go get your bride" (the modern equivalent of the same). At that point, the bridegroom would lead a small group, including his male attendants, back to the bride's house at night, with torches to light the way.

The bride would not know exactly when this would happen but would have a good idea, as we see her pictured in the Scriptures waiting and making ready with her maidens (young virgins). The shout would be heard: **"Behold, the bridegroom is coming; go out to meet him!" (Matthew 25:6),** and the entire group, the entire wedding party, would return to the father's house. This second step, the return of the bridegroom, is clearly illustrated in the parable of the ten virgins in Matthew 25:1–13.

The third step is the marriage supper. Just as today's wedding receptions vary from relatively small affairs to huge banquets, marriage suppers in Israel could be short or could go on for days, as was illustrated by Jesus turning water into wine at the wedding at Cana (John 2:1–10).

The Marriage Supper of the Lamb is beautifully pictured in the book of Revelation in heaven, just prior to the second coming of Jesus and the return to earth with the bride of Christ.

> *6 And I heard, as it were, the voice of a great multi-*
> *tude, as the sound of many waters and as the sound*
> *of mighty thunderings, saying, "Alleluia! For the Lord*
> *God Omnipotent reigns! 7 Let us be glad and rejoice*

and give Him glory, for the marriage of the Lamb has come, and His wife has made herself ready." 8 And to her it was granted to be arrayed in fine linen, clean and bright, for the fine linen is the righteous acts of the saints. 9 Then he said to me, "Write: 'Blessed are those who are called to the marriage supper of the Lamb! And he said to me, "These are the true sayings of God." (Revelation 19:6-9)

As I mentioned earlier, an appropriate appreciation of the Marriage Supper of the Lamb provides a vivid picture of Christ's redemptive work and His bride, the church. The three steps of the wedding process are fully operative in the life of the individual believer.

The first step takes place when we place our faith in Jesus Christ as our Lord and Savior. This is the commitment that is made, and the indwelling of the Holy Spirit is the proof of the commitment made by God. There was a dowry paid as well, and that was the sacrifice of Jesus and the blood of the Lamb of God shed for the forgiveness of sin. The entire body of Christ, also known as the church, is the bride, waiting for the return of the bridegroom. We have been promised; we are the betrothed.

The second step, as mentioned above, is described in the parable of the ten virgins in Matthew 25:1–13. This is a parable but, at the same time, a very tightly associated foretelling of the rapture of the church. While not knowing the day or the hour of His return, the bride is to remain attentive and wait. Saved by grace, the bride is to be chaste and remain holy while waiting for the bridegroom. Paul's letter to Titus expresses it this way:

11 For the grace of God that brings salvation has appeared to all men, 12 teaching us that, denying ungodliness and worldly lusts, we should live soberly, righteously, and godly in the present age, 13 looking for

the blessed hope and glorious appearing of our great
God and Savior Jesus Christ. (Titus 2:11-13)

The Apostle Paul calls this appearance of the bridegroom *"blessed hope."* Like a modern wedding, along with the bride and groom, there are others in attendance, including the Old Testament saints and the tribulation martyrs. In verse 9 above, the angel says, *"Write: 'Blessed are those who are called to the marriage supper of the Lamb!'"*

The actual marriage feast, the third step in the wedding process, occurs in heaven at some point during the seven years of tribulation. John sees it and writes about it in Revelation 19, just before the second coming, but it can actually take place at any time during the seven years. Some scholars speculate that it happens at the beginning of the tribulation and actually lasts seven years, a correlation to the Hebrew tradition of *Shiv'at Y'mei Mishteh,* a seven-day wedding feast said to have been instituted by Moses.

While we could say that most modern weddings are really all about the bride, the Marriage Supper of the Lamb is really all about the bridegroom! However, in reality, there is no marriage without both a bridegroom and a bride. The image presented of the marriage supper that takes place in heaven just before the second coming is not symbolic or purely spiritual, but physical. It happens after the bodily resurrection of every believer, who is then presented to the risen Savior and Lord, Jesus Christ, who is called the bridegroom.

The wedding garments are white linen, which every believer will be given:

And to her it was granted to be arrayed in fine linen,
clean and bright, for the fine linen is the righteous acts
of the saints. (Revelation 19:8)

The Marriage Supper of the Lamb is a key piece to fully understanding the unique role of the body of Christ, the sufficiency of His atonement on the cross for our sins, and this present church age that comes to a close at the rapture, the resurrection of the body of Christ.

Soon after the close of this present age, which we discussed in chapter eight, a seven-year countdown begins to its ultimate fulfillment in the *Second Coming of Jesus Christ.* Do not miss this gospel truth: Jesus is coming back again! His return is eminent. The prophetic promises revealed in Sacred Scripture demand it. Often, we look around and think that things are falling apart. In reality, things are falling into place. Events, nations, kings, armies, and alliances are all marching forward according to God's ultimate plan.

And God's ultimate plan includes Jesus ruling from Jerusalem on the throne of David. All of the prophecies related to the glorious reign of the Messiah will be fulfilled. He will establish His kingdom in Israel and rule and reign over this earth. The Bible clearly tells us that we, that is, the body of Christ, will rule with Him for 1,000 years. This is called *"The Millennium."*

CHAPTER TWENTY-THREE
THE MILLENNIUM

Seven years after the tribulation begins, Jesus returns in glory! His return is not to be taken allegorically or merely spiritually, as some believe, as Jesus Christ's literal second coming to earth is referenced three times more often than His first coming in the Bible, including by Jesus Himself. When we read the prophecy in Micah that Bethlehem is to be the birthplace of the Messiah, we have no problem understanding the literal fulfillment of that prophecy and believing the historical fact that Jesus was born in Bethlehem. In the very same way, there are many other unfulfilled prophecies regarding Israel and the coming kingdom, and they will be fulfilled literally as well.

Just as importantly, the Bible teaches that Jesus' return, His second coming, is not the end but, in many ways, the beginning. Many, if not most, of the hundreds of unfulfilled prophecies will be fulfilled after Jesus returns in what is called the Millennium. Millennium is an English word taken from the Latin word *mille*, which means *"thousand."* The belief that Jesus Christ reigns on earth for one thousand years comes primarily from the twentieth chapter of Revelation, and the two words *"thousand years"* are mentioned six times in the first seven verses of the twentieth chapter of Revelation.

While there is much to discuss regarding the Millennium, let's first look at the first ten verses of the twentieth chapter of Revelation to get the appropriate context. I'll also underline the six references.

1 Then I saw an angel coming down from heaven, having the key to the bottomless pit and a great chain in his hand. 2 He laid hold of the dragon, that serpent of old, who is the Devil and Satan, and bound him for a <u>thousand years</u>; 3 and he cast him into the bottomless pit, and shut him up, and set a seal on him, so that he should deceive the nations no more till the <u>thousand years</u> were finished. But after these things he must be released for a little while.

4 And I saw thrones, and they sat on them, and judgment was committed to them. Then I saw the souls of those who had been beheaded for their witness to Jesus and for the word of God, who had not worshiped the beast or his image, and had not received his mark on their foreheads or on their hands. And they lived and reigned with Christ for a <u>thousand years</u>. 5 But the rest of the dead did not live again until the <u>thousand years</u> were finished. This is the first resurrection. 6 Blessed and holy is he who has part in the first resurrection. Over such the second death has no power, but they shall be priests of God and of Christ, and shall reign with Him a <u>thousand years</u>.

7 Now when the <u>thousand years</u> have expired, Satan will be released from his prison 8 and will go out to deceive the nations which are in the four corners of the earth, Gog and Magog, to gather them together to battle, whose number is as the sand of the sea. 9 They went up on the breadth of the earth and surrounded the camp of the saints and the beloved city. And fire came down from God out of heaven and devoured them. 10 The devil, who deceived them, was cast into

*the lake of fire and brimstone where the beast and the
false prophet are. And they will be tormented day and
night forever and ever. (Revelation 20:1-10)*

I mentioned back in chapter one of this book that the first key to
understanding prophecy was to *"take the literal meaning when practical!"* However, there are many who do not take the prophecy of a
thousand years literally. This unfortunate teaching that the thousand
years, mentioned six times, are not to be taken literally is called **amil-
lennialism**. And, while this is not heresy and was actually held by much
of the church for about 1,000 years (interesting and ironic, don't you
think?) there are many of us who teach a more literal approach to Bible
prophecy, including the thousand years, also known as the Millennium.

Now that we have identified some terms, let us look again at what
the twentieth chapter of Revelation teaches.

- **Satan is imprisoned for 1,000 years.** The Scriptures tell us
  Satan is the adversary, and he is locked away. The words used
  in the verse include *tied up, threw it into the abyss, locked, and
  sealed,* indicating the full cessation of the devil's schemes and
  influences. For the next thousand years, both nations and individuals will be free of his influence and temptations.

- **The sentence is limited!** God is faithful to fulfill His promises,
  and the thousand years are when they are accomplished! After
  the thousand years are over, Satan will once again deceive the
  nations. *"Now when the thousand years have expired, Satan
  will be released from his prison." (verse 7)*

- **Two resurrections precede the great white throne judgment.**
  Two resurrections are foretold, the first for the just, the second
  for the unjust. The just, including the tribulation saints that
  were martyred and the old testament saints, are resurrected and

reign with those that were resurrected prior to the tribulation. The resurrection of the unjust leads to the great white throne judgment at the end of the 1,000 years: ***"And I saw the dead, small and great, standing before God, and books were opened. And another book was opened, which is the Book of Life. And the dead were judged according to their works, by the things which were written in the books." (verse 12)***

- **The saints reign with Christ for a thousand years.** In their resurrected bodies, both the Old Testament and New Testament saints reign with Christ, fulfilling the words of Jesus in the parable in Matthew 25:34. ***"Then the King will say to those on His right hand, 'Come, you blessed of My Father, inherit the kingdom prepared for you from the foundation of the world."***

- **Satan is judged and sentenced.** At the end of a thousand years, Satan is released one last time. Despite living in a genuine paradise on earth, Satan is able to deceive the nations, and they rise with Gog and Magog as their leaders and surround the holy city, where the saints also reside. This rebellion is short-lived, as fire comes down from heaven and destroys them. Satan is judged and sent to the Lake of Fire to join the beast and the false prophet.

The Revelation of Jesus Christ was, in all likelihood, one of the very last books of the New Testament and was written by the Apostle John on the island of Patmos between 90 and 95 AD. Within a few years, some of the early church fathers were already quoting passages from Revelation and commenting on the thousand years to come.

For example, Papias of Hierapolis, the Greek Apostolic Father and Bishop (60 AD–130 AD), is said to have known the Apostle John. He was the prolific author of many commentaries on the gospels, the ministry of Jesus in Galilee, and the history of the early church, including the deaths of the Apostles James and John. He wrote passionately of *"a certain millennium after the resurrection"* and that there would be a corporeal reign of Christ on this very earth. Irenaeus, a second-century bishop, not only wrote of a literal thousand-year reign but also of a gloriously rebuilt Jerusalem.

The Old Testament has much to say about the Millennium and the glorious reign of the Messiah, the Prince (i.e., Daniel 9:25). There is so much information provided by the prophets and in the book of Psalms that it is easy to see why the Jewish people were hoping that Jesus would bring about the fulfillment of these promises during His first advent. One of the things we need to realize is that the Jewish people were not wrong; the Messiah is going to rule and reign on the throne of David! They were just unaware of the coming dispensation of grace, which was a mystery that the Apostle Paul says was supernaturally revealed to him.

> *2 If indeed you have heard of the dispensation of the grace of God which was given to me for you, 3 how that by revelation He made known to me the mystery (as I have briefly written already, 4 by which, when you read, you may understand my knowledge in the mystery of Christ), 5 which in other ages was not made known to the sons of men, as it has now been revealed by the Spirit to His holy apostles and prophets. (Ephesians 3:2-5)*

After this present time period, known as the "Age of the Church," the prophecies of the Old Testament prophets will be fulfilled. For example, many scholars see the tribulation, the second coming, and the millennial reign of Jesus all referenced in Psalm 2. The first part of the psalm speaks of an uprising, a conspiracy to revolt against God and His anointed. However, the Lord laughs and has this to say about the second coming and the millennial reign of the Messiah:

8 Ask of Me, and I will give You
The nations for Your inheritance,
And the ends of the earth for Your possession.
9 You shall break them with a rod of iron;
You shall dash them to pieces like a potter's vessel.' "

10 Now therefore, be wise, O kings;
Be instructed, you judges of the earth.
11 Serve the Lord with fear,
And rejoice with trembling. (Psalm 2:8-11)

As the prophecies of the glorious reign of Jesus Christ do not use the term *"a thousand years"* or the word *"millennium,"* it is easy to miss the timing of when these things are to occur. Nevertheless, the holy Scriptures do contain sufficient information about the coming Millennium, along with an absolute assurance that it will come. Here's an extended passage found in the Book of Isaiah:

5 Then the eyes of the blind shall be opened,
And the ears of the deaf shall be unstopped.
6 Then the lame shall leap like a deer,
And the tongue of the dumb sing.
For waters shall burst forth in the wilderness,
And streams in the desert.
7 The parched ground shall become a pool,
And the thirsty land springs of water;
In the habitation of jackals, where each lay,
There shall be grass with reeds and rushes.
8 A highway shall be there, and a road,
And it shall be called the Highway of Holiness.
The unclean shall not pass over it,
But it shall be for others.
Whoever walks the road, although a fool,

Shall not go astray.
9 No lion shall be there,
Nor shall any ravenous beast go up on it;
It shall not be found there.
But the redeemed shall walk there,
10 And the ransomed of the Lord shall return,
And come to Zion with singing,
With everlasting joy on their heads.
They shall obtain joy and gladness,
And sorrow and sighing shall flee away. (Isaiah 35:5-10)

There are many other passages in the Bible in which we learn what life will be like in the Millennium; however, there is not one place we can go for an overview other than what we have already listed from Revelation chapter 20. However, here are a few highlights of the Millennium, in no particular order.

1) All People Will Be Strong and Healthy

What governments and modern science have failed to do, the Lord will accomplish during the Millennium. The prophet Isaiah again has this to say: "*Then the eyes of the blind shall be opened, And the ears of the deaf shall be unstopped. 6 Then the lame shall leap like a deer, And the tongue of the dumb sing. For waters shall burst forth in the wilderness, And streams in the desert*" (Isaiah 35:5-6).

The Bible tells us that prior to the flood, people lived a lot longer than they do today. Adam lived to 930 years, Seth to 912, and Enosh to 905! After the flood, the average lifespan was significantly reduced; however, Abraham lived to be 175 (Genesis 50:26) and Moses to be 120 (Deuteronomy 34:7). A verse in Psalm 90 sums up pretty much our present lifespan: "*The days of our lives are seventy years; And if by reason of strength they are eighty years, Yet their boast is only labor and sorrow; For it is soon cut off, and we fly away*" (Psalm 90:10).

Some believe that the reason for renewed health and vitality for those living in mortal bodies (unlike the resurrected saints that will never die) may be a result of new diets or new natural medicines. However, the easiest explanation is the eradication of diseases (heart disease, diabetes, and cancer) that have been a curse and will be removed in the Millennium.

2) Jerusalem Becomes the Capital City of the World

Jesus reigns as King of Kings from Jerusalem, and all peoples and nations come to Jerusalem for instruction and to embrace the law (Isaiah 2:3). The Angel Gabriel told Mary about the son in her womb: *"He will be great, and will be called the Son of the Highest; and the Lord God will give Him the throne of His father David. 33 And He will reign over the house of Jacob forever, and of His kingdom there will be no end." (Luke 1:32–33)*. King Solomon extended the borders of ancient Israel north to the Euphrates River (including modern-day Syria, Iraq, Iran, and Lebanon) all the way to the border of Egypt. This entire area will again be returned to Israel as her inheritance and for the settlement of the returning twelve tribes. During the Millennium, the hill on which Jerusalem presently sits will become a mountain that towers over all other mountains (Isaiah 2:2). Since Revelation 16:20 tells us that both the mountains and islands disappear, the Lord will do some supernatural work on Israel and likely on other former mountain ranges after the devastation of the tribulation.

3) The Disbandment of All Armies and the Destruction of All Weapons of War

A bronze statue of a man holding a hammer in one hand and a sword in the other, hammering the sword into a ploughshare, stands in front of the United Nations in New York City. The statue, a gift from the USSR to the United Nations in 1959, symbolizes the verse depicting the millennial reign of Jesus Christ from the book of Micah:

> *He shall judge between many peoples,*
> *And rebuke strong nations afar off;*
> *They shall beat their swords into plowshares,*
> *And their spears into pruning hooks;*
> *Nation shall not lift up sword against nation,*
> *Neither shall they learn war anymore. (Micah 4:3)*

4) The Earth Will Be Repopulated

While the resurrected saints will not be given in marriage and will not have any more children (Luke 20:35), mortal humans that survive the tribulation, both Jews and Gentiles, will be more than capable. Because the Bible teaches that in the Millennium, people will live a very long time (Isaiah 65:20) and that children will play in the streets of Jerusalem (Zechariah 8:4), we can expect that over those 1,000 years, the population of the earth will again grow to billions of people. The prophecy given in Revelation is our proof text. Scripture tells us that at the end of the tribulation, when Satan is again released from his prison, he *"will go out to deceive the nations which are in the four corners of the earth, Gog and Magog, to gather them together to battle, whose number is as the sand of the sea" (Revelation 20:8).*

5) Ezekiel's Temple Finally Will Be Built

Both Jewish and Christian scholars have marveled at the vision Ezekiel had around 575 BC of a glorious temple. At that time, Solomon's Temple in Jerusalem had been destroyed, and Ezekiel recorded an amazing vision of a magnificent and enormous temple that we read in Ezekiel chapters 40–48. While two more temples have been built in

Jerusalem—Zerubbabel's temple and then the same one expanded by Herod—neither has been built to the grand dimensions given to Ezekiel.

As this temple has not yet been built, the fulfillment of the vision that Ezekiel had must be in the future and, in all likelihood, will be the temple that is built and will be in service during the Millennium. I mention this as my last example of a highlight of the Millennium for two reasons. First, the size of Ezekiel's temple is massive, much larger than the present temple mount in its entirety. Secondly, Ezekiel's Temple is part of the vision of dry bones and the ultimate regathering of the people of Israel, shown below:

> *25 Then they shall dwell in the land that I have given to Jacob My servant, where your fathers dwelt; and they shall dwell there, they, their children, and their children's children, forever; and My servant David shall be their prince forever. 26 Moreover I will make a covenant of peace with them, and it shall be an everlasting covenant with them; I will establish them and multiply them, and I will set My sanctuary in their midst forevermore. 27 My tabernacle also shall be with them; indeed I will be their God, and they shall be My people. 28 The nations also will know that I, the Lord, sanctify Israel, when My sanctuary is in their midst forevermore." (Ezekiel 37:25-28)*

CHAPTER TWENTY-FOUR
Afterword—The Blessed Hope

We started this conversation, this book on the Apocalypse, with the reminder that Jesus taught us to pray, *"Thy kingdom come, thy will be done."*

Have you ever prayed that prayer? It's a simple prayer; many children memorize it by the time they are old enough to go to school, before they even learn how to read. The words "Thy kingdom come" indicate that God's kingdom is not yet entirely fulfilled. It's likely that many, if not most, of those who pray that simple yet profound prayer are unaware of His coming kingdom. Many are unaware that at any moment, the trumpet of God may sound, and Jesus will return to fulfill His promise to return: *"And if I go and prepare a place for you, I will come again and receive you to Myself; that where I am, there you may be also" (John 14:3).*

"Thy kingdom come" also acknowledges that God is sovereign, and we who pray that prayer must fully submit to His authority, His rule, over our lives. Our faith believes in the promise that Jesus will come back. Hopefully, this book has clearly convinced you and all who read it that Jesus will come back for those who have received Him, for those who have called upon His name, and are living for Him.

The Bible makes it very clear that you can be assured that Jesus is coming back for you! There is no need to fret or worry over your eternal security. Christianity is not so much a religion as it is a relationship with God through Jesus Christ. He paid the penalty for our sins on

Calvary. He was the spotless Lamb of God whom the Apostle John saw and recorded in his vision in the book of Revelation. (Revelation 5:6.) Jesus' sacrifice on Calvary, once and for all, provides full atonement for your sins.

The Apostle Paul wrote more than one-quarter of the entire New Testament. His epistle to the Romans is an amazing letter that teaches how our sins separate us from a loving God. Paul clearly explains how we cannot possibly make ourselves right or earn salvation on our own. But we need salvation; we need to be saved, for the Apostle Paul tells us, *"For all have sinned and fall short of the glory of God" (Romans 3:23).*

In His loving kindness, God provided a way to redeem and save us, and that was only through His Son, Jesus Christ. Paul's epistle to the Romans gives us the good news! Paul writes, *"For the wages of sin is death, but the gift of God is eternal life in Christ Jesus our Lord" (Romans 6:23).*

While there is no formula or method that fully produces a pathway to salvation like a Betty Crocker recipe, the Apostle Paul gives us a promise that we can hold onto. He writes, *"if you confess with your mouth the Lord Jesus and believe in your heart that God has raised Him from the dead, you will be saved. 10 For with the heart one believes unto righteousness, and with the mouth confession is made unto salvation" (Romans 10:9–10).*

You may think, "That sounds too simple!" And many end up either delaying making this commitment to faith in Jesus Christ or trying to add other things to that simple promise. Please do not delay! Do not wait until tomorrow what you can acknowledge today. To repent means to "change directions" or "change your mind." You can repent and agree with God that Jesus is Lord! Jesus was born in order to live a perfect life and die on the Roman cross as a sacrifice for sin. Three days after He died on the cross for your sins, He rose from the dead. That needs to be the confession of every person who calls himself or herself a Christian. Allow the Holy Spirit to enter your life and begin to change you from within. Jesus is coming, and you'll want to be ready when He comes!

About the Author

Dr. Kenneth A. Behr is the host and president of Faith Dialogue Inc., whose mission is to equip the body of Christ, promote the unity of the church, encourage pastors, and strengthen churches. Pastor Behr is an educator, theologian, pastor, and best-selling author. He is the founder and senior pastor of Celebrate Seniors, a church that embraces the older generation, restores dignity, promotes a healthy spiritual life, provides spiritual growth opportunities, and ministers as well to the families of these senior adults.

He has been a pastor and executive pastor in some of the largest churches in the country and served previously as president of the ECFA, headquartered in Washington, DC. Ken and his wife Carol have been married for over 40 years and have two children and five grandchildren. He has spent the last 20 years in ministry and was ordained by the Evangelical Church Alliance after a career in business.

CPSIA information can be obtained
at www.ICGtesting.com
Printed in the USA
BVHW050951270623
666446BV00009B/53